RESCUING THE
WORLD BANK

RESCUING THE WORLD BANK

A CGD WORKING GROUP REPORT AND SELECTED ESSAYS

Nancy Birdsall, ed.

CENTER FOR GLOBAL DEVELOPMENT
Washington, D.C.

Rescuing the World Bank: A CGD Working Group Report and Selected
Essays may be ordered from the Center for Global Development.
Contact: publications@cgdev.org.

Library of Congress
Control Number: 2006932977
ISBN-10: 1-933286-11-3
ISBN-13: 978-1-933286-11-2

Printed in the United States of America
Cover design: Grammarians
Typesetting by LanguageWorks
Printed by United Book Press, Inc.
Baltimore, Maryland

Nancy Birdsall is the founding president of the Center for Global Development. Before launching the Center, she was the senior associate and
director of the Economic Reform Project and the Carnegie Endowment
for International Peace. Birdsall was previously executive view president
of the Inter-American Development Bank and director of the World Bank's
research department. She is the author, co-author, or editor of more than
a dozen books and monographs.

Rescuing the World Bank: A CGD Working Group Report and Selected Essays

Preface to
Rescuing the World Bank
A CGD Working Group Report
and Selected Essays

The development and transformation of societies where poverty and disease afflict large numbers of people is a central challenge of the 21st century. In broad terms at least, that point, once agreed, seems to justify the existence of the World Bank—still possibly the single best-placed institution to address that challenge.

But the World Bank has been under siege—assailed by critics of the left, right and center on grounds it is not effective, not accountable, not democratic or legitimate, and most threatening of all for the Bank, no longer relevant in a global economy where private capital, production and ideas dominate.

Yet the world does need a strong World Bank. Without reform and revitalization at the Bank agreed by its members—the advanced economies and the poorest—the world will have one less institution to manage not only "development" in the conventional sense of the word, but the related global challenges of the 21st century.

Are the Bank's current shortcomings exaggerated, or are they potentially fatal, marking a moment that will later be seen as the start of a long decline into irrelevance and obscurity? If they are potentially fatal, can this critical institution be rescued?

For the most part the contributors to this book see the Bank as an institution at risk—in a way it has not been before—but one that can be rescued. Readers will find here different positions on the what, why and wherefore of the Bank's current weaknesses—and on what exactly ought to be done with what priority to rescue it. These differences notwithstanding, the book is packed with practical suggestions that the shareholders (the Bank's 184 member governments) and the president of the Bank can take to move their institution toward greater strength, flexibility, and effectiveness in a rapidly changing global economic system.

This book has two parts. The first dates to the appointment of Paul Wolfowitz as the new president of the Bank in the spring of 2005. We at the Center for Global Development saw the logic of drawing up an agenda for him, in support of anticipated efforts to revitalize the Bank. The Working Group we organized focused not on internal management issues but on the structural changes—in mandate, instruments, and its own governance—that are critical to a renewed Bank. The group defined five tasks on which the president should exercise leadership in persuading the Bank's member governments to take action. The report of the group, *The Hardest Job in the World: Five Crucial Tasks for the New President of the World Bank*, was made available to President Wolfowitz on his official entry to the Bank on June 1, 2005. It is presented in its original form here as part one of this monograph. To my mind, the tasks remain as crucial today as they were when the report was first issued.

The second part has its roots in the September 2005 Annual Meetings of the IMF and the World Bank in Washington D.C. To generate healthy discussion and debate and to explore the recommendations with a broader community, including officials and private sector actors attending the Annual Meetings, the Center organized a symposium on the Friday preceding the weekend meetings. We were fortunate to have President Wolfowitz himself kick off the symposium by thanking the Center and the members of the Working Group for their effort—and noting that if his job was not the "hardest" in the world it was certainly the "best". The second part of this volume comprises a set of essays largely based on the presentations made that day to a large and enthusiastic audience.

Readers of the essays will note substantial differences between some authors on some issues. That was the point of the symposium and is the point of this publication—to contribute to the healthy discourse on a set of difficult issues with no easy answers. In that sense, this volume represents the kind of contribution the Center for Global Development strives to make on the many difficult issues confronting the development community today.

I would like to extend my thanks to three groups of people who were responsible for bringing this volume to life.

The first is the team responsible for *The Hardest Job in the World*. We were fortunate to convince a small group of 18 distinguished colleagues—from the private sector, academia, civil society, and the governments of rich and developing countries—to come together over the course of three months to map out an agenda for the new president. I was particularly fortunate to have Devesh Kapur, a CGD non-resident fellow (now at the University of Pennsylvania) and co-author of *The World Bank: Its First Half Century*, an authoritative two-volume history of the Bank, join me in chairing the group. His encyclopedic knowledge of the Bank and his creative insights were a priceless asset to our work. The work of the Working Group was coordinated by Milan Vaishnav, my former special assistant who is now a graduate student at Columbia. As in every other task, he was superb, bringing a steady hand and fine judgment to every step of the process.

In addition, many others who could not participate in the group also provided input and comments, including Masood Ahmed, Jessica Einhorn, Ravi Kanbur, Maureen Lewis, Johannes Linn, Peter McPherson, and John Sewell. In particular, I would like to thank Kemal Dervis (former CGD visiting fellow who is now head of the United Nations Development Programme), John Hicklin (also a former CGD visiting fellow, while on sabbatical from the IMF), and David Peretz (former U.K. executive director at the Bank and IMF) for their extensive comments on the draft.

Second, I thank the participants of the Annual Meetings symposium and other authors whose work appears as essays in the second part of the volume. Without their willingness to review and revise, and their patience, we would have missed a unique opportunity to showcase the thoughtful and provocative analysis and recommendations of some of the world's foremost experts on the World Bank.

Last, but certainly not least, I thank heartily Lawrence MacDonald and his outstanding communications and publications staff for their support in the production of this volume.

I hope that this book will contribute to the growing momentum for change at the World Bank. Change seems crucial to me and other contributors to this volume. Only by changing to meet the demands of the 21st century can the World Bank live up to its potential to be a powerful, positive force for greater and more broadly shared prosperity.

Nancy Birdsall
President
Center for Global Development
June 1, 2006

A CGD WORKING
GROUP REPORT

Preface to
The Hardest Job in the World: Five Crucial Tasks for the New President of the World Bank

The Center for Global Development has a special interest in the World Bank. Compared with the Bank, we are a small institution. But our mission is virtually the same—to reduce poverty and inequality, to maximize the benefits of globalization for developing countries and their poor, and to improve people's lives. That is no accident. I am myself a former World Bank staff member who looks back with pride and satisfaction on the opportunity the Bank gave me to contribute (modestly, for sure) to that grand mission, and almost all of my colleagues here have similar experience and missionary zeal about the great development project. With the advantage of complete independence, we do research and engage actively on how the rich world and the global institutions—including the World Bank—can better affect the poor world. At our launch in November 2001, we were honored by the presence of James Wolfensohn, then in his sixth year as World Bank president, who framed it very well indeed, saying, in all good humor, that he hoped we'd be tough on him and on the Bank.

It was natural then, when we learned in February of James Wolfensohn's departure from the Bank, to begin thinking about the risks and the opportunities his successor would face. I asked a small group of distinguished colleagues—from the private sector, academia, civil society, and the governments of rich and developing countries—to join a working group to discuss and make recommendations addressed to the new president. I was fortunate to persuade Devesh Kapur, a non-resident fellow of the Center (now at Harvard) and the co-author of the authoritative book on the World Bank's history, that he should join me in chairing the group. Without his help, his insight, and his patience, this report would not be what it is.

3

Members of the working group met three times. First in February 2005, shortly after the candidacy of Paul Wolfowitz was announced. Second in March and finally in late April. This report would not have been possible without their willingness to contribute their time, their energy, and most important their good wisdom and good judgment to our deliberations. Along with Devesh, I thank them enormously for their interest and dedication, their insights, their issue notes, and their continuous stream of thoughtful comments on working drafts. Many others who could not participate in the group also provided input and comments. We especially thank Masood Ahmed, Jessica Einhorn, Ravi Kanbur, Maureen Lewis, Johannes Linn, Peter McPherson, and John Sewell.

Our thanks go also to three others. Kemal Dervis, a non-resident fellow of the center, was named the administrator of the United Nations Development Programme in the middle of our deliberations. He played a key role in shaping our deliberations from the inception of the group, especially on issues of the Bank's role in global economic governance. John Hicklin, a visiting fellow at the Center on leave from the International Monetary Fund, participated in the group's discussions and consultations in his personal capacity and provided thoughtful comments on a range of issues. The perspective offered by David Peretz, formerly a senior U.K. Treasury official and executive director of the Bank and the Fund, was also invaluable.

Finally, my own thanks go above all to my companion-in-arms and special assistant Milan Vaishnav. He is at the beginning of what will surely be a long and successful career. He brought his own good questions, political insights, and instinctively good judgment to our project, as well as critical attention to detail and timeliness. He was, above all, patient with my bad habit of last minute changes at late hours. Without colleagues at the Center, especially Lawrence MacDonald and his superb team, and Gunilla Pettersson, Milan and I could not have crossed the finish line.

Readers of our report will see that Working Group members started from a shared assumption: that the world needs a strong World Bank. A central challenge of the 21st century is securing sustainable growth and poverty reduction in the developing world, where five of every six people live today (and eight of every nine will live in less than 50 years). The Bank is perhaps the world's single best-placed institution to address that challenge. To do so effectively, the Bank needs to change however, adapting quickly its mid-20th century policies and habits to the greatly changed global environment.

Our Working Group focused not on internal management issues but on the structural changes—in mandate, instruments, pricing, and its own governance—that are critical to a revitalized Bank. We look to Mr. Wolfowitz to take bold leadership in pushing for those changes through cajoling and consensus-building with the Bank's member governments. We look to the Bank's many constituents, including civil society groups concerned with social justice around the world, to support him in pushing for those changes. The challenge now belongs to him to exploit the potential of what we call, with good reason, the hardest job in the world. We hope this report helps guide him in that challenge.

Nancy Birdsall
President
Center for Global Development
June 1, 2005

The Hardest Job in the World: Five Crucial Tasks for the New President of the World Bank

Executive Summary

This report sets out five crucial tasks for the World Bank president to tackle over the next five years. They are tasks for which the president—through a combination of charm, cajoling, and horse-trading—must corral the Bank's recalcitrant collective of member governments, including its single largest shareholder, the United States, to take action—action critical to securing the Bank's credibility, legitimacy and effectiveness for the 21st century.

The five tasks are informed by a set of guiding principles on which members of the Working Group agree (see box).

Guiding Principles for the New President

- *The Bank's mission and in-country priorities.* The Bank's agreed mission (reducing poverty through equitable growth) provides no real guidance on country-specific priorities. It is time to end the confusion between what is good for development in general and what the Bank itself should do in a particular setting. In today's complex donor system, the Bank need not do everything everywhere. It should take leadership on the idea of partnership with a country's own and with other international efforts.

- *Equitable growth and political savvy.* Rich-country support for the Bank demands that the Bank's engagement and financing in borrowing countries leverage policies be pro-poor and supportive in general of a more secure and sustainable global system. But such "leverage" cannot rely on the detailed conditionality of a "nanny Bank." It must rely on Bank staff's being politically savvy—sensitive to a country's political constraints and to the opportunities of responsible leaders to push reforms. That implies a premium on systematic analysis of local politics and institutions—and on increasing Bank-wide research and analysis of country governance.

7

> • *The Bank as development's brain trust.* The Bank's singular comparative advantage is its staff's broad-ranging knowledge and experience on the full range of technical, sectoral and economic issues of development. The resulting brain trust cannot be unbundled from the Bank's financing role, however. It is lending that triggers and supports policy dialogue and advice to countries, and it is the income from lending that helps finance the brain trust.
>
> • *The Bank's governance: toward greater legitimacy and effectiveness.* The Bank's legitimacy and effectiveness going forward require that its borrowers be better represented in its governance. It should undergo a transformation from a development agency to something closer in spirit to that of a global "club" in which today's developing-country beneficiaries, not only its rich-country benefactors, have a keen sense of ownership and financial responsibility.

The five priority tasks are:

• Revitalize the World Bank's role in China, India, and the middle-income countries.
• Bring new discipline and greater differentiation to low-income country operations.
• Take leadership on ensuring truly independent evaluation of the impact of Bank and other aid-supported programs.
• Obtain an explicit mandate, an adequate grant instrument, and a special governance arrangement for the Bank's work on global public goods.
• Push the Bank's member governments to make the Bank's governance more representative and thus more legitimate.

Revitalize the World Bank's Role in China, India, and the Middle-Income Countries

Borrowing from this group of countries has declined dramatically, because of the high "hassle" costs of dealing with the Bank and because of their increasing (though at times uncertain and costly) access to private capital markets. Their reduced borrowing puts at risk the Bank's maintenance of its global expertise, its ability to leverage equitable and sustainable policies, and its net income over the long run. To remain relevant for these countries, whose participation in the global club matters for global progress, the Bank must transform the way it does business. The new president should:

- Ask the shareholders to review the charter to determine if the provision that International Bank for Reconstruction and Development loans be guaranteed by a sovereign borrower has stifled the Bank Group's ability to catalyze private investment, lend to municipal and other nonsovereign entities, support deepening of local capital markets, and in general respond more effectively to the changing demands of its key borrowers, especially for its more active and strategic involvement in catalyzing local and foreign investment.
- Find ways to sharply expand the range of financial products and instruments now available to borrowers, such as products and instruments to hedge against commodity and other risks, better use of the guarantee function, and, by the Bank itself borrowing in local currency or in a mix of emerging market currencies, making it possible for countries to borrow from the Bank in their own currency.
- Create a new loan product that would visibly reduce hassle costs for creditworthy countries with reasonably good performance in economic management and an adequate record of enforcing environmental and other safeguards.
- Introduce differential pricing among International Bank for Reconstruction and Development borrowers, tied strictly to per capita income (not to credit rating), to encourage less borrowing for the right reason— ushering in de facto "graduation" without any arbitrary rule-based loss of access.
- Explore other pricing or product innovations that would create incentives for borrowers to make their own public revenue collection and expenditures more progressive (without sacrificing growth).

Bring New Discipline and Greater Differentiation to Low-Income Country Operations

Support for an expanded Bank role in low-income countries is broad-based. At the same time there are widespread doubts about its past effectiveness in these countries, many of which have weak governments and limited absorptive capacity, and failing to grow much in the past, acquired unsustainable debt burdens. The new president should:

- Signal support for a much more differentiated approach depending on each country's governance, in terms of the size and types of transfers, with longer-term commitment periods for the best-performing countries and much more flexibility in reducing transfers ("exit") when progress stalls, while maintaining robust administrative spending to sustain policy dialogue and engagement and technical assistance in all countries independent of the size of transfer programs.
- Urge the shareholders to formalize a third, fully grant-based window for countries with very low per capita incomes, for example, below $500; most of these are countries whose poor record of growth implies little capacity to take on debt.
- Work with the International Monetary Fund on an agreed role for the Bank in signaling the adequacy of a country's "development" approach and on a facility to protect selected International Development Association countries against external shocks.

Take Leadership on Ensuring Truly Independent Evaluation of the Impact of Bank and Other Aid-Supported Programs

Although the Bank has improved its level of transparency through its research and the increasingly frank and systematic work of its internal evaluation department, neither satisfies the need for a credible, truly independent assessment of the impact of development investments. Echoing calls from the Meltzer Commission, the Overseas Development Council Task Force on the Future of the

IMF, and the Gurría-Volcker Commission for independent evaluation across donors, the Working Group recommends that the president:

- Take leadership in working with the board to support the creation of an independent evaluation entity financed and governed by a consortium of public and private donors and recipient countries, to complement current internal audit and evaluation activities.

Obtain an Explicit Mandate, an Adequate Grant Instrument, and a Special Governance Structure for the Bank's Work on Global Public Goods

Over the years, the Bank has been drawn into the financing and provision of a multitude of global programs ranging from the environment to public health. The result is a situation in which the Bank has a set of *ad hoc* global programs without a clear mandate from its shareholders and without the grant instrument needed for its more effective engagement in provision and financing of high-priority global public goods. The Working Group recommends that the president:

- Call on the shareholders to develop a clear mandate for the Bank's role in the financing and provision of global public goods.
- Initiate and maintain an ongoing dialogue with the regional development banks, the United Nations, and other relevant agencies to develop the proper division of labor for respective work on global and regional public goods.
- Call on shareholders to create a Global Public Goods Trust Fund to finance the Bank's work on global public goods, based on agreed annual transfers from the Bank's net income and on contributions from non-borrowers. Propose a governance structure for the trust fund ensuring at least 40 percent representation of middle-income and emerging market economies (whose borrowing contributes to net income) and 10–20 percent representation of International Development Association countries.

Push the Bank's Member Governments to Make the Bank's Governance More Representative and Thus More Legitimate

The Bank's own governance fails to adequately represent the contribution and the interests of its borrowing members. The lack of adequate representation is undermining its legitimacy and puts its effectiveness at risk. Yet there is no issue that has been as impervious to change. The president should:

- Request that the governors of the Bank discuss and formalize a mechanism for choosing the Bank's next president that is credible, rule-based, and transparent.
- Support establishing two additional seats on the board for African countries, pending a larger consolidation to fewer restricted board seats.
- Ask the Bank governors to call for an independent and public assessment of voting shares and board representation, including assessment of the merits of double-majority votes on selected issues and taking into account discussion in the current quota review at the International Monetary Fund of its quota allocation.
- Ask the governors to commission a time-bound independent review of board functions and responsibilities, with an eye toward increasing its overall effectiveness in holding Bank management accountable.

The Hardest Job
in the World

Paul Wolfowitz assumes the presidency of the World Bank at a key moment for the Bank and for the development community. The Bank, as the world's premier institution for development, is to play a big part in the success of a revitalized global consensus—formalized in 2000 by more than 150 heads of state at the United Nations—to halve global poverty and to reach many other Millennium Development Goals by 2015. Why? Because of its financial strength and because of the breadth and depth of its staff's expertise on a wide range of development issues.

Conflicting demands from mutiple quarters make it impossible to keep all con-stituencies happy

But the Bank faces some real challenges in adapting its internal governance structure and instruments—put in place 60 years ago—to dramatic changes in the global economy and in the relative power and needs of its shareholders. The rise of China, the creation of a European Union, the dramatic increase in private capital flows to developing countries, the new risks of AIDS and global terrorism—all are telling examples.

As a public institution, the Bank relies on the financial and political support of its government members— and, in the new global environment, of many other constituencies and "stakeholders." Yet conflicting demands from multiple quarters make it impossible to keep all constituencies happy.[1] It is thus an easy target. Those on the left accuse it of protecting privileged insider financial and corporate interests—and perpetuating the influence of the United States and other G-7 members rather than the world's poor people and their civil society supporters. Those on the right accuse it of misusing public resources in emerging markets where private markets could operate better—and creating aid dependency in the poorest countries where its loans have contributed to unsustainable debt.[2]

The poorest countries, especially in Sub-Saharan Africa, have called on the Bank to dramatically increase its operations to help them meet the Millennium Development Goals. Yet inside as well as outside its walls, there are

13

serious concerns about its effectiveness in the many poor countries whose state systems are still weak or, worse, corrupt. Meanwhile Bank operations are declining in China, India, and the big middle-income economies, as they borrow less and less. But the Bank's mainstream lending to these countries is what sustains its in-house expertise and helps finance its administrative budget, some of its poor country programs, and many of its nonlending activities.

The biggest challenge for the Bank's new president will not be managing the Bank but providing global leadership in the fight against poverty

Ironically, because of its financial resources and its in-house management and expertise, the Bank's members expect it to respond to multiple demands to do everything, from assessing post-conflict reconstruction needs in Kosovo and Iraq to developing a pilot program for trading carbon emission rights across borders, to coordinating closely with other donors and the United Nations on the Millennium Development Goals. Simultaneously, its management is accused of "mission creep."[3]

No surprise, then, that the Bank is under pressure. Its legitimacy, its credibility, its effectiveness, and its fundamental mission are all in question—as is its future stream of support and income. In his decade as president, James Wolfensohn managed several of those pressures quite deftly. But without agreement of the Bank's member governments to fundamental changes in its governance and the instruments at its disposal, he could not address them all.

The Bank's new leader needs to be ambitious. He faces an unusual risk—for all the Bank's strengths, merely continuing with business-as-usual risks undermining its future. He also faces an unusual opportunity—to provide global leadership in advancing the global development project. In the Bank's self-effacing bureaucratic parlance, global leadership is called "working with the shareholders"— the Bank's "shareholders" are the nations of the world.

This report defines a forward-looking agenda for the new World Bank president to tackle over the next five years. Its recommendations focus on five crucial tasks. They are tasks for which the president—through a combination of charm, cajoling, and horse-trading—must corral the Bank's recalcitrant collective of member governments, including its single largest shareholder, the United States, to take action—action to strengthen and secure the Bank's credibility, legitimacy and effectiveness for the twenty-first century.

Guiding Principles

The five recommendations in this report are informed by the following guiding principles.

The Bank's mission and in-country priorities

The Bank's mission is to reduce poverty in developing countries. The most effective path to poverty reduction is economic growth that is equitable enough to reach poor people. Growth should also be sustainable (in the environmental sense), and, to be sustained over time, driven by private sector investment. On these points there is no real disagreement.

But a statement of the Bank's mission does not alone provide guidance on its own operational priorities (where "operations" refer not only to loans and grants, but also to "dialogue" and advisory services). In today's complex donor system, the Bank need not and should not do everything everywhere. But without a clear mandate to set country priorities, history and habit suggest that Bank staff will continue doing just that—limited only by borrowers' willingness and ability to borrow.[4] Although the Bank naturally provides advice and loans in a wide variety of areas across countries, it needs to be clear on its own priorities within individual countries—often in the complicated context of other donor programs. That means ending the confusion between what is good for development in general (such as girls' education) and what is good for equitable and sustainable growth in a particular country at a particular time (where and when it might be rural roads that have the highest marginal benefit—even for encouraging girls' education). And it means setting priorities for what the Bank itself should do in each country; even when the Bank is the single agency with the broadest overall knowledge of a country's development needs (which is often but not always the case), it need not be the largest financier of development investments.

Compounding the lack of clear operational priorities in countries is a new round of uncertainty about the ingredients of growth that can reduce poverty. Under pressure from critics, Bank staff in the 1990s interpreted the "poverty" mission as a mandate to lend directly for poverty reduction. Combined with the pressures of safeguards against environmental abuse in infrastructure projects and the growing concerns about corruption in the procurement process for large projects, the poverty emphasis led to a shift of lending toward the social sectors. In the last year or so, in marked contrast, there is renewed talk of infrastructure as a priority, as a quicker path to "growth" (and through growth to poverty reduction) than social spending, and as less vulnerable to the bottlenecks that management and human resources limits put on rapid expansion of health and education systems.[5]

The development community has learned that no single recipe or set of priorities to achieve poverty-reducing growth can be applied across countries. On the one hand there is broad consensus on the prerequisites of sustained growth ranging from the importance of human capital, in particular health and education, of macroeconomic stability, and of institutions and governance. But chastened by heterodox China's spectacular growth, reformist Latin America's dangerous vulnerability to external volatility, and Sub-Saharan Africa's embarrassing accumulation of unsustainable debt, the development community and the Bank are less confident about how precisely to operationalize broad, widely agreed upon goals, in particular settings. Put another way, there is no longer anything that could be called a "Washington Consensus," nor across all Bank borrowers, any simple choice of encouraging more infrastructure versus more social investment.[6] There is, at best, a growing consensus that sound institutions—political and economic—matter and that institutions have to be invented locally, tailored to local political and social realities. That puts a premium on respect for and partnership with local efforts by Bank staff, and on the need for country-specific knowledge and expertise.[7]

Equitable growth and political savvy

The new emphasis on local institution building and local ownership raises an additional challenge for the Bank. Ownership and the loss of faith in any universal policy package imply that the Bank should become less of a "nanny" Bank, preoccupied with the detailed conditionality and structural reform demands that dominated lending in the late 1980s and much of the 1990s. It should instead concentrate more on supporting healthy local economic and political institutions. But local political ownership in developing countries (indeed in all countries) is not necessarily conducive to equitable or pro-poor growth.

The Bank's engagement and financing in borrower countries is supposed to leverage policies that are equity-enhancing and public spending that is pro-poor. The result is tension between a nanny Bank exercising leverage and a politically naïve Bank overdoing country ownership.

The Bank's future effectiveness depends on managing that tension well. That implies much more attention to identifying and quantifying corruption risks, interest group pressures, and other local political constraints (and opportunities). It means helping to lead multilateral efforts to combat bribery (such as the Extractive Industries Transparency Initiative). And it means setting operational priorities that take those risks into account.[8] It implies an approach that is both politically sensitive and politically savvy.

It also means increasing the resources for data collection, measurement, and analysis of corruption, transparency, the rule of law, the business environment, and so on across countries. All this is necessary for the Bank to be a global brain trust addressing the difficult politics (and economics) of growth that is pro-poor.

The Bank should concentrate more on supporting healthy local economic and political institutions

The Bank as development's brain trust

External resources are mainly fungible, and the Bank need not and should not be the primary source of development finance (either because other donors provide major resources in poor countries or because government revenue and private capital provide the bulk of resources in middle-income and fast-growing emerging markets). The implication is the need to distinguish clearly between the Bank's role in transferring financial resources and its particular comparative advantage: its singularly overarching overview of global opportunities, institutions, and constraints, and of borrowers' institutional and financial capacity. That overview is grounded in broad-ranging and deep staff knowledge and experience on technical, sectoral, and economic issues. No other institution has the same strength in the generation and diffusion of knowledge about the practice of development. (Indeed, as a "knowledge bank," creating and sharing across countries development experience and expertise, the World Bank itself constitutes a global public good—an institution that no one country today would have sufficient incentive to create or fund, yet from which all potentially benefit.)

The knowledge bank will be handicapped if not supplemented by two additional efforts. First, it must do more to create capacity for knowledge generation in borrowing countries. The Bank cannot be a substitute for independent policy thinking in borrowing countries—this tendency has fueled the perception of a parochial and arrogant institution. Second, it must make much greater efforts at disseminating knowledge—as a knowledge clearinghouse—for example, by such apparently basic steps as making its website more multilingual.[9]

Strengthening the brain trust requires the Bank to retain its financing role

The Working Group acknowledged that strengthening the brain trust requires the Bank to retain its financing role. The lending process often triggers and supports the policy dialogue and advice to countries, reinforcing the Bank's capacity as a brain trust. Advice not linked to finance too often ends up on ministry bookshelves. The income from lending also augments the resources to support the institution's advisory function.

The Bank's governance: toward greater legitimacy and effectiveness

The Working Group's recommendations look toward a transformation of the Bank from a development agency—in which some members are financial contributors and others are beneficiaries—to something closer in spirit to that of a global "club." In a global club today's developing country beneficiaries, not only its rich country benefactors, would have a keen sense of ownership and financial responsibility. Such a transformation would recognize that the Bank cannot be effective and relevant in addressing major global economic problems if countries such as Brazil, China, India, South Africa and Turkey are not full members with corresponding rights and responsibilities.

The Working Group also noted that improving the Bank's governance was only part of the larger challenge of building a more legitimate and effective overall system of global governance, encompassing the Bretton Woods institutions, the regional banks, the World Trade Organization, and the United Nations. Improved World Bank governance should thus be seen as part of broader and deeper reforms of the existing international architecture. The World Bank and the International Monetary Fund (IMF), in particular, must work to build a more constructive and effective partnership, not only with each other but also with the United Nations.

Five Crucial Tasks
Drawing on these guiding principles, the Working Group
identified five crucial tasks for the new president. These
tasks are not meant to be comprehensive. They are tasks
where the president's leadership is needed to guide and
shape decisions by the Bank's member governments
and where the absence of leadership risks undermining
the Bank's contributions going forward. The five crucial
tasks are:

- Revitalize the Bank's role in China, India, and middle-income countries.
- Bring new discipline and greater differentiation to low-income country operations.
- Take leadership on ensuring truly independent evaluation of the impact of Bank and other aid-supported programs.
- Obtain an explicit mandate, an adequate grant instrument, and a special governance arrangement for the Bank's work on global public goods.
- Push the Bank's member governments to make the Bank's governance more representative and thus more legitimate.

A transformation of the Bank from a development agency to something closer in spirit to that of a global "club"

Revitalize the World Bank's Role in China, India, and the Middle-Income Countries
The Bank's role in middle-income countries and in such
low-income but fast-growing emerging markets as China
and India can no longer be taken for granted. The majority
report of the International Financial Institution Advisory
Commission (mandated by the U.S. Congress in 2000
and commonly referred to as the "Meltzer Commission"
for its chairman, Allan Meltzer) recommended that the
Bank stop lending to emerging market economies and
middle-income countries with ready access to private
capital markets.[10]

Many of the Bank's fast-growing and middle-income
borrowers seem to share this view. The long-term trend of
their borrowing from the Bank is clearly down, especially
from the exceptionally large outflows of the Bank in the
late 1990s during the financial crises that hit East Asia,
then Russia, and then Brazil and Argentina. Bank staff and
country officials generally take the view that the decline
reflects reduced demand from borrowers, not reduced
willingness to lend.[11]

Why lend to countries with access to private capital?

The Working Group concluded, in contrast, that the World Bank should continue to be active in middle-income countries and in such emerging markets as China and India.[12] There are at least three reasons: many of these countries' limited access to private capital markets, the legitimate interest of the Bank's rich members in encouraging pro-poor, equitable growth policies in middle-income and emerging market economies, and the logic and evident success of past "bundling" of policy advice with loans.

The World Bank should continue to be active in middle-income countries and in such emerging markets as China and India

Easing limited access. Even for the large countries that are deemed attractive to investors, private capital markets (internal and external) are still volatile and pro-cyclical. For the poorer middle-income countries (such as Guatemala, Kazakhstan, and Paraguay) as well as those where internal conflicts persist (the Philippines and Sri Lanka) and domestic debt is high (Brazil and Turkey), access to external capital is still largely limited to shorter-maturity loans. For these and other richer economies in this category access to internal capital is often costly due to relatively weak and shallow banking systems, small, illiquid local capital markets, and the risk that too much sovereign borrowing in thin domestic market will make banking systems more vulnerable.[13] In almost all of the Bank's middle-income borrowers, only time and performance—much more than a decade of steady, sound economic policies—and the visible resilience of economic and political institutions will induce domestic and foreign creditors and investors to accept lower returns for their capital in return for lower country risk.

Experience shows, moreover, that the cost and availability of funds in international markets can change abruptly, sometimes for reasons beyond the control of any country. In the process, economic growth, development strategies, and antipoverty programs may suffer setbacks. When global turmoil partially or completely closes market access, multilateral lending can assist in sustaining adequate public spending on education and health, in strengthening regulatory and supervisory capacity, and in developing social safety nets—as in Mexico in 1995 and the Republic of Korea in 1998. Since crises tend to hurt the poor the most through lost employment and income and interrupted education for children, assisting countries in coping with crises helps alleviate poverty and promote development. When the Bank maintains and even increases lending during periods of stress, it signals support for responsible development policies, and with relatively modest amounts helps rebuild market confidence.

In the meantime, longer-term and cheaper loans from the World Bank can encourage public investments with high social and economic returns that do not yield commercial returns to private agents (such as investments in education, health, rural infrastructure, bank regulation, and judicial reform) and that otherwise might not find a place in national budgets. These are investments that, by supporting equitable growth in open market systems, create an environment that crowds in productive private investment.[14]

Promoting equitable growth. Even putting aside volatile, crisis-prone access to capital, advanced economies have an interest in reducing poverty in developing countries and in investing in human resources. The Working Group noted that more than two-thirds of the world's poor lives in middle-income and emerging market countries. China and India alone account for 45 percent of the total. Pro-poor and human development instruments yield high returns but only in the medium term, and countries with weak tax systems cannot easily translate the economic returns for a road into the tax revenue to repay short-term loans.[15] The social and economic decisions of middle-income countries affect the health and well-being of their own peoples, undermining or advancing such global goals as poverty reduction.

Moreover, the United States and other nonborrowing members have a substantial security stake in the institutional resilience of middle-income and emerging market economies. Their financial stability contributes to global financial stability. And their decisions—on commodity and energy use, international capital market borrowings, reducing corruption, and so on—affect the once-insulated residents of rich countries. For that reason nonborrowing members also have a legitimate interest in encouraging middle-income and emerging market economies to invest in programs that generate global and country-specific benefits.

Lending operations are a vehicle for supporting and rewarding policy reforms and development results...

Bundling policy advice with loans. Lending operations are a vehicle for supporting and rewarding policy reforms and development results. And there are good reasons to doubt that unbundling the financing from the "dialogue" about policy and results would always be effective (though it may make sense for some countries). The Bank does and should continue to charge for advisory services, proving the worth of its stock of expertise. However, political and social constraints in emerging markets, as well as technical complications, make it difficult to design and implement many reforms—for example of health, banking systems, bankruptcy law, and pension and unemployment programs. Officials from such countries as Brazil, Hungary, the Republic of Korea, Mexico, Thailand, and Turkey repeatedly cite the services bundled with Bank financing as a key reason for seeking Bank loans. They cite the leverage that the potential financing provides them within their own political settings as helpful in persuading and encouraging progress on their reform agenda. They value not only the dialogue on tough internal policy and budget choices that the lending process catalyzes but also the detailed, project, sectoral, and economic analysis by Bank staff.[16]

Services bundled with lending also support objectives of the global community: human development, protection of the environment, financial accountability, and standards of public procurement that curtail corruption and promote competition. For example when Bank financing supports general government expenditure, the accompanying dialogue and advice promote better debt management and responsible budget management. Put another way, lending is the vehicle for the Bank, by supporting reformers within government, to influence governance issues (accountability of government, and greater representation of all citizens in economic decisionmaking) and contribute to strengthening democratic institutions in emerging market economies.

Then why are these countries borrowing less and less?

What lies behind the decline in the demand for Bank loans? Despite the below-market interest rates and long maturities of Bank loans, the trend in the last 15 years has been for middle-income borrowers to reduce their new borrowing from the Bank. In some cases, countries have prepaid loans whenever the cost of borrowing on the private market has been low. For fiscal years 1990–97, International Bank for Reconstruction and Development (IBRD) lending, measured by gross disbursements, was in the range of $15–18 billion (figure 1). There was a brief spike in response to the Asian financial crisis, but in fiscal 2004 lending dropped to the $10 billion mark. As a result, for many middle-income borrowers, net transfers from the Bank are now negative.

...and by supporting reformers within government, strengthening democratic institutions in emerging market economies

To some extent, this trend is healthy. Some one-time borrowers (Hungary, the Republic of Korea, Malaysia, Singapore, and Thailand) have graduated from Bank borrowing—though some returned when hit by the global financial problems of the late 1990s. To some extent, the emerging market economies' vulnerability to global financial volatility has led to a tougher standard on acceptable external debt-to-GDP ratios for such countries—as low as 40 percent—which has reduced demand for external borrowing in general. But developing countries should generally be net importers of capital not exporters. (The illogic of negative net transfers from the Bank is repeated and dramatized in the illogic of some emerging markets accumulating large dollar reserves.)

It is also true that the Bank appears to be succumbing to the broader problems rather than compensating for them, and that officials of the middle-income countries and emerging market economies have additional reasons, more Bank-specific, for their declining demand for Bank loans. One is the limitations of the Bank's longstanding main product: the sovereign guaranteed loan, compared

Figure 1 IBRD Lending, Fiscal 1995–2004
$ billions

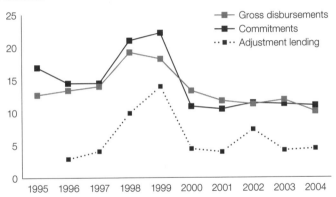

with the range of innovative financial products available in the private market. A second is the high "hassle" or transaction cost (not the financial cost) of borrowing from the Bank, compared with the small and declining difference in cost of borrowing from private markets in recent years.

Within the World Bank Group, the International Finance Corporation (IFC), the Multilateral Investment Guarantee Agency (MIGA), and the Foreign Investment Advisory Service (FIAS) do supplement the IBRD's sovereign-guaranteed loans with lending, equity investments and advisory services, primarily to private sector agents. But it is still an uphill battle to see any common strategic direction built into country programs of these various arms of the Bank Group. And the fact remains that the financial capacity and the balance sheet of the IBRD are much larger than those of the IFC, and the membership and the financial clout of MIGA and FIAS remain limited. As a result, the World Bank Group continues to lag behind in the range of its products, and the IBRD has limited means to make meaningful its allegiance to private sector growth, since its main instrument requires a sovereign guarantee.

For example, the IBRD does offer partial risk guarantees as well as loans.[17] But because the IBRD's financial policies require that these guarantees be priced and provisioned in virtually the same manner as loans, the guarantee is not as attractive to the countries as a loan, and demand for it has been close to zero. In addition, the Bank's guarantees also require a sovereign counterguarantee. But the requirement for a counterguarantee violates the reasonable requirement of responsible central governments to avoid backing up subsovereign borrowing.

Similarly, the IBRD cannot make loans to municipal and other subsovereign governments without a formal guarantee of the central government—which as with guarantees many governments now eschew, since such guarantees undermine the accountability of nonsovereign political entities and thus the healthy development of disciplined local government. (The regional development banks do not have the requirement for the sovereign guarantee built into their charters, and in the last decade they have begun to offer a broader range of products, including those for subsovereign and private borrowers. As a result, the World Bank Group may be losing its longstanding position of leadership in analysis and innovation.)

In short, credit products come in forms other than loans, and the Bank could add more value for some of its borrowers by going up the credit-product value chain (just as commercial players have done with their—more limited—appetite for emerging market risk). New credit products could also have more of an insurance element to them, insuring against such market-related risks as movements in interest rates, foreign exchange rates, and commodity prices, which the private sector structures and distributes, but for which their credit appetite is limited.[18]

The "hassle" problem that discourages borrowing includes the long lapse of time between a government's initiating a loan request and getting the loan approved, the onerous administrative burden of preparing, negotiating, and implementing Bank-financed programs and projects, and the administrative and financial costs of dealing with the growing demands of the Bank—often pushed by well-meaning civil society groups in the advanced economies—that borrowers meet high environmental and other standards in the design and implementation of Bank-financed projects. Whether these standards are "too high" is a matter of controversy. That they raise the perceived if not actual costs of projects and can slow down their approval and implementation is undoubted.[19]

The Bank could add more value for some of its borrowers by going up the credit-product value chain

Without the very large and fast-disbursing "adjustment" loans to countries during the Asian financial crisis, to Brazil in 1999, and to Argentina in 2000–01 to supplement IMF balance of payments support, the Bank's net income from its "bread and butter" loans would be even lower. Indeed, one reason countries prefer adjustment loans is that they dramatically reduce up-front "hassle" costs, and they eliminate the resource and reporting burden of the "counterpart" funds that countries are usually required to provide from their own budgets for conventional projects. With the requirement for such counterpart funds, the Bank also compromises its effectiveness as a countercyclical lender, which would otherwise help countries minimize the social costs of economic downturns.

Why does it matter?
The demand for borrowing from this set of countries may on current trends remain low and fall further—despite

the benefits to the borrowers and despite the legitimate security and development interests of nonborrowers in the Bank's continuing engagement with those countries. Over the next decade, a rapid exit of more creditworthy borrowers poses three additional risks to the Bank: a severe adverse selection problem in the Bank's portfolio, reduced net income, and lost opportunities for the Bank to transfer experience from middle-income countries to low-income countries as they develop.

Major changes are needed in the operations of the Bank if it is to be effective and relevant in middle-income countries

The Bank's own cost of borrowing might rise slightly if its creditors saw greater portfolio risks, reducing the financial benefits to the very countries still in most need of Bank financing. Equally problematic for all the Bank's members would be a reduction in its net income—its income from the spread between its cost of borrowing and the interest earned on its loans. Low demand from the Bank's IBRD borrowers risks undermining not only its potential positive role in middle-income countries but also the financial strength on which its other roles—in low-income countries, in transferring cross-country experience, in providing advice, and in supporting the provision of global public goods—at least partly depend (figure 2). It also risks reducing the ongoing internal learning and knowledge-generating role of Bank staff, who learn in an active lending program.

We conclude that major changes are needed in the operations of the Bank if it is to be effective and relevant in this group of countries. Our recommendations to the new president for China, India, and the middle-income countries are as follows:

1. Ask the shareholders to begin a systematic and careful review of whether the charter requirement that IBRD loans be guaranteed by a sovereign borrower has stifled the Bank Group's ability to respond to the changing demands of its key borrowers.

   Could it be that the separate balance sheets of the IFC and the IBRD, for example, have discouraged the development of new products to catalyze private sector investment in middle-income and emerging market economies? Does the IBRD charter make it too difficult for the Bank to lend to municipal and other subnational and other subsovereign government entities?

Whether or not the outcome of any such review would lead to structural changes, the Working Group believes it would open the door to new thinking about the medium-term instruments that the Bank and other multilateral development banks need to be responsive to the key problems and changes in the global economy.

2. Find ways, within current constraints, to sharply expand the range of financial products and instruments now available to borrowers. It is widely acknowledged that the Bank has been extremely innovative when it comes to its own borrowings and investments. But it has been anything but innovative in its own product offerings, which remain almost entirely concentrated on the single-priced sovereign guaranteed loan. Examples of possible new products and related new approaches include:

Find ways to sharply expand the range of financial products and instruments now available to borrowers

- Risk management products and instruments to hedge against commodity risk. (In emerging market economies the private sector has little appetite for providing these services, and the Bank could step in to fill a clear void.) Risk-sharing loan contracts could tie the rate of interest on sovereign loans to commodity export prices, especially for countries heavily dependent on primary commodity exports.
- Leveraging the Bank's financial strength and shedding the undue conservativeness that have

Figure 2 IBRD Net Income: Sources and Uses, Fiscal 2004

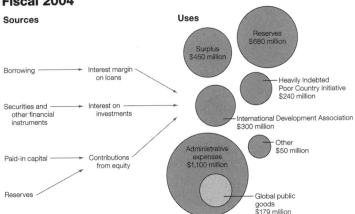

Sources

Borrowing ——→ Interest margin on loans

Securities and other financial instruments ——→ Interest on investments

Paid-in capital ——→ Contributions from equity

Reserves

Uses

Surplus $450 million

Reserves $680 million

Heavily Indebted Poor Country Initiative $240 million

International Development Association $300 million

Other $50 million

Administrative expenses $1,100 million

Global public goods $179 million

made Bank guarantees no more attractive than loans, while tightening the distinction between guaranteeing political risk, which the Bank should do, and commercial risk, which it should avoid.

- Borrowing in local capital markets to help strengthen these markets and lending in the local currency (ideally long-dated, fixed-rate, and indexed to local price levels so that the debt cannot be inflated away) to help borrowers avoid the currency risk that borrowing from the Bank usually entails.

Create a new loan product that would visibly reduce hassle costs for selected borrowers

- Developing other products to help borrowers reduce their currency risks. The Bank could, for example, borrow in a synthetic unit whose value was determined by a basket of inflation-indexed emerging market currencies, and sell bonds denominated in this unit to international investors. The Bank would cover itself against exchange risk by on-lending the borrowed money to countries in their own currencies (on an indexed basis, in the proportions that make up the basket).[20]

- Working with the IMF to explore still other possibilities, for example, on how Bank lending could contribute to refinancing the sovereign debt of overindebted middle-income countries (at marginally more than the Bank's borrowing rate and ideally in a country's own currency), in return for continuing, monitored progress on disciplined macroeconomic priorities.[21]

3. Create a new loan product that would visibly reduce hassle costs for selected borrowers.

The effect of the profusion of project safeguards and program conditionalities on quality may be driving away some borrowers, particularly from interest in large infrastructure projects. For borrowers with reasonably good performance in economic management and an adequate record and regulatory effort in procurement, environmental protection, and human rights, the Bank should move to a more arm's length relationship. The Working Group recommends that the Bank develop a new instrument that would greatly reduce the hassle cost for creditworthy countries that are vulnerable when, for example, new investments require resettling of people in new locations.

An existing facility—the "deferred drawdown option"—is a start in this direction, but has not been attractive to borrowers because it is not clear that it would be sufficiently automatic. We recommend that the Bank develop few and well defined standards of eligibility, developed in consensus with all members, and that the list of countries with eligibility for one-stop access be updated periodically. Terms of eligibility could be revisited and redefined every three years or so. The reduction in the "hassle factor" would not only increase the demand for Bank loans—even assuming a higher borrowing rate for eligible countries—but would also reduce the Bank's administrative costs. The latter savings, as we argue later, would yield substantially greater social returns if deployed in the financing of global public goods.

Add a degree of differential pricing among IBRD borrowers, tied strictly to per capita income

Not all middle-income countries will meet the eligibility requirements for such hassle-free lending, and we are certainly not suggesting that only countries that are high-performing be eligible for any loans (as with the U.S. Millennium Challenge Account). The Bank should continue to take risks in middle-income countries where resources have a reasonable probability of being used effectively and where conventional monitoring and conditionality can increase that probability.

4. Add a degree of differential pricing among IBRD borrowers, tied strictly to per capita income (not to credit rating), recognizing that the implicit benefit to less creditworthy borrowers is already larger than to more creditworthy ones.

A marginally higher rate for richer countries with better credit ratings would encourage less borrowing for the right reason—ushering in de facto "graduation" without any recourse to arbitrary rule-based loss of access.[22] It would also, like the facility proposed earlier, create incentives within the Bank to reduce hassle costs for the somewhat better-off middle-income countries—some of which are now fully capable of preparing and managing large loans for electricity distribution, agricultural research, and health systems.

5. Explore other pricing or product innovations that would create incentives for borrowers to make their own public revenue collection and expenditures more progressive (without sacrificing growth)—and that would encourage investments with a high payoff for global public goods.[23] Starting from a country borrowing rate based on per capita income, loan charges could be reduced for large ramp-ups in expenditures on financially high-risk but clearly pro-poor sectors, such as basic education and health, rural roads, training recipient country nationals, and other long-term capacity building.

In most middle-income and emerging market economies, there is no tradeoff between the government's fiscal behavior being more equitable and at the same time more efficient. Indeed, fairer and more equitable revenue and expenditure patterns would be more efficient—for example, because public spending on health and education of reasonable quality increases worker productivity, and because reduced tax evasion and lower trade and payroll taxes are both pro-poor and growth enhancing.[24] Because resources are fungible, clear rules on the increment to the proportion of government budgets to be eligible for this kind of incentive would need to be developed. This approach would also require clear rules of country eligibility.

Bring New Discipline and Greater Differentiation to Low-Income Country Operations

Support for a strong and even expanded Bank role in low-income countries is broad-based. This is especially true for Africa, particularly in the context of the 2005 U.N. Millennium Review Summit (which will evaluate progress toward the Millennium Development Goals) and the United Kingdom's call to address Africa's problems at the 2005 G-8 Summit in July. Reflecting that support, rich-country contributions to the Bank's International Development Association (IDA) window increased from $13 billion in the 13th replenishment to $18 billion in the 14th, and bilateral foreign aid commitments from Europe and the United States have surged in the last several years.

Discipline and differentiation

Broad support for the Bank's engagement in helping low-income countries achieve the Millennium Development Goals should not obscure concerns about the Bank's and other donors' effectiveness in those countries. These concerns range from the difficulty of avoiding imposing ideas and recipes (as reflected in the view that Poverty Reduction Strategy Papers still reflect countries' expectation of what the Bank wants more than their own priorities) to the difficulty the Bank and other donors have in "exiting," in reducing their transfers when countries are not using external help well.[25]

Donors are making substantial efforts to increase their coordination and harmonize their approaches in low-income countries, many of which receive aid from dozens of bilateral and multilateral agencies as well as international nongovernmental organizations (NGOs). The Bank, often the most influential among many donors, needs to set the tone—creating space for countries to manage their own priorities wherever that makes sense, cooperating with others in helping countries set clear priorities, and ensuring in its own operations more discipline and differentiation in the amount and nature of support it provides, depending on recipient countries' capacity, governance, and economic management.

This will require substantive changes in the way the Bank does business. The Bank, with its vast array of expertise on a wide set of issues, coupled with its decentralized structure, has tended to encourage strategies and programs on a wide set of initiatives, with no sense of which are the most important.[26]

But most governments in low-income countries simply do not have the capacity to tackle a very wide agenda. Governments with very scarce time, money, and skilled staff need to set priorities, which in practice usually means deciding which issues will not be dealt with right away. The Bank, as one of many partners, including the relevant regional development bank, U.N. agencies, bilateral donors, and international and local nongovernmental organizations—should have a broad strategic role advising a country on its priorities—combined with what should often be a narrow focus for its own lending.

The Bank should also take more of a lead in helping donors discriminate across low-income countries in the amount and nature of their transfers. The discussion in recent years about "country selectivity" has led to the idea of providing large sums of money to well-governed countries that can use it well and less to poorly governed countries (the U.S. Millennium Challenge Account's approach). But well-governed countries should not only receive more money, they should receive it in more attractive ways that give them more substantive input, responsibility, and certainty about future funding. The Bank has moved tentatively in this direction by funding Sector-Wide Approaches and introducing Poverty Reduction Support Credits in certain countries. But these different approaches should become more formalized.

The Bank should take more of a lead in helping donors discriminate across low-income countries

In less well-governed countries, the Bank should be much more modest—limiting its lending and limiting its expectations. It should not reduce its engagement, its budget for policy dialogue and technical assistance, or its willingness to take certain risks. On the contrary, the administrative budget for poorly performing countries should be explicitly untied from the program of lending or grants. But the Bank should be more prepared to suspend financing where that makes sense and to design programs that build in such suspensions when progress stalls.

Specifically, the Bank should have three distinct strategies for low-income countries, depending primarily on the quality of the recipient's governance.[27]

1. *Low-income better governed countries.* The Bank should provide large amounts of financing to these countries, delivered mostly in the form of budget support or program aid. Along with other donors, it should focus less on micromanaging activities and more on measuring and achieving broad results. The Bank should commit funding for five years or more in these countries, subject to the strict requirement that recipients show continued good governance and achieve reasonable results.

2. *Low-income countries with average governance.* These countries should receive less funding than the better-governed countries. The Bank should be more involved in setting priorities and ensuring broad-based participation and technical rigor. Strengthening public financial management is usually a very high priority in these countries, and to strengthen reforms in this area some budget support may be appropriate. Most funding should, however, be for well-designed projects

or sector support consistent with the country's overall development strategy, focusing on key activities where achieving results seems most likely, well integrated with country budgeting and financial management arrangements. The length of financial commitments should be shorter than for well-governed countries, perhaps three to five years, contingent on progress and results. Performance should be monitored carefully in these countries, with clearly delineated performance standards. Strong performance and improved governance should lead to increased financial support, a shift to budget and sector support, and longer commitments—while weak results should lead to less aid.

3. *Low-income poorly governed countries.* These countries, broadly consistent with the Bank's "Low-Income Countries Under Stress" must be dealt with carefully case-by-case, because circumstances on the ground can vary widely and change quickly. Some are failed states, others are failing, still others are weak or fragile. Some donors (but probably not the Bank) should direct significant amounts of aid to civil society groups and NGOs.[28] The Bank should continue with substantial engagement and carefully targeted technical assistance, but should not generally be providing financing to government. It should not get into retail-style grantmaking to civil society groups because its comparative advantage is in working directly with governments.

In less well-governed countries, the Bank should be prepared to suspend financing and to design programs that build in suspensions when progress stalls

Grant financing
Differentiation on the amount of resource transfers should be based primarily on country governance. Another kind of differentiation—for the type of transfer (grant or loan)—should be based on countries' per capita income. Since President Bush proposed that 50 percent of IDA funds be used as grants in July 2001, there has been a strong debate about the extent to which the Bank should provide grants rather than loans to low-income countries. The rationale for IDA shifting to greater use of grants is the past accumulation of unsustainable official debt by many low-income borrowers, including debt to the World Bank. Much "new lending" prior to debt reduction was simply helping countries repay former loans.

The Bank's members should agree to formalize a third, fully grant-based window for countries with very low per capita incomes, for example, below $500

Negotiations between the United States and the Europeans (who were concerned about the effects of reduced future reflows for IDA's finances) led to an initial fuzzy compromise during the IDA-13 replenishment in 2002. The Bank's Board decided that 18–21 percent of IDA funds would be grants for a smorgasbord of purposes: post-conflict reconstruction, natural disasters, HIV/AIDS, education, health, water, and sanitation. This led to a less-than-satisfactory outcome in which countries would receive grants for some activities and loans for others. Recognizing these problems, the Board amended the guidelines in March 2005 to make debt sustainability the basis for the allocation of grants. While an improvement, the arrangement is less than ideal. Using debt sustainability as the basis for grants introduces moral hazard issues (countries that have taken on more debt in the past will now receive grants, while those that have not must continue to borrow). It also creates administrative problems (doing country-by-country assessments of what portion of grant financing each country should receive).

Instead, grant allocations should be based primarily on income levels following the same principles that now guide the allocation between IBRD and IDA loans. The Bank's members should agree to formalize a third, fully grant-based window for countries with very low per capita incomes, for example, below $500, an average income just over the $1 day poverty line.[29] The logic is straightforward: loans make sense when the recipient's economy can grow fast enough to generate the resources to repay the loans. But most countries with incomes below $500 have never achieved sustained economic growth—not for hundreds of years. Until they achieve such growth, grants make far more sense than loans. Moreover, the very poorest countries are least able to cushion themselves against shocks, making it more difficult to repay loans, even following good investments. Given very scarce resources, any funds generated by strong investments should be re-invested locally, not repaid to the Bank.

Extending the IDA horizon for recipient countries, while encouraging "exit" when appropriate
Donors agree that for poor countries to meet the Millennium Development Goals requires an increase not only in the

amount of aid but also in its predictability and horizon over a longer period. Responsible finance ministers in the poorest countries naturally hesitate to hire new teachers and build new schools where the prospect of financing their ongoing costs from the country's own revenues is limited, while external funds are volatile and uncertain over the medium term. The Bank through its IDA window should be more able and willing to make longer-term commitments to the best-performing countries—as long as 10 years—contingent on continuing progress against clearly defined benchmarks.[30] The time horizon for development in IDA countries is, after all, still 40–50 years. Consider Mozambique, with per capita income of about $210. With very robust annual per capita income growth of 5 percent, it would take almost 30 years for Mozambique to reach the IDA operational cutoff of $865 per capita.

The Bank should be more able and willing to make longer-term commitments to the best-performing countries

The Bank could extend the predictable horizon of its commitments. But it often errs in the opposite direction—prolonging commitments and programs when countries are not meeting agreed benchmarks of progress or are backsliding on human rights, on friendly business environments, on expenditure management, or on other measures of governance. Part of the problem is the periodic pressure on Bank management, as a result of the IDA three-year replenishment cycle, to fully commit its resources. Alternatives should be explored to reduce that pressure. For example, IDA recipients and nonborrowers could agree on having a portion of unused IDA contributions going directly to a trust fund for global public goods (see below) or rolling them over into the next cycle. The effects of any changes along these lines could then be reviewed for subsequent decisions on the next cycle.

Relations with the IMF in low-income countries
There has been significant discussion within the IMF in recent years about the changing its role in low-income countries. With the resolution (for the most part) of the macroeconomic crises that plagued many low-income countries in the 1980s and early 1990s, the IMF's financial role is likely to diminish over time. Consideration is thus being given to new modalities for it to monitor and signal the strength of macroeconomic policies without direct financial involvement—in the form of "unfunded

programs" or other "policy support mechanisms." This implies that the Bank's complementary role in judging the strength of country medium-term development strategies will become more important—including in assessing for other donors the appropriate level and composition of overall support. This will be the case irrespective of the size—relative to that of other donors—of the Bank's financial involvement in a particular country.

This puts a greater onus on the Bank—if it is to maintain its credibility in countries where it is also providing financial transfers—to make sufficiently independent judgments on a country's policy and institutional status. The new president should initiate a discussion with shareholders and the donor community on the criteria for judging a country's development strategy and on how the Bank's views should most effectively be signaled.

The Bank should work with the IMF to make selected IDA countries eligible for automatic additional transfers in the event of an external shock

Dealing with external shocks

Many IDA countries are particularly vulnerable to external shocks, be it weather, a commodity price shock, or a sudden collapse of the economy of a critical trading neighbor. In principle, the IMF should help countries adjust to shocks. But it does not have any grant facility. The Bank should thus work with the IMF on a facility to make selected IDA countries at very low income levels eligible for automatic additional transfers in grant form. Short-term but rapidly disbursed transfers could be tied to preselected programs primarily of a social insurance nature—say, to fund the recurrent costs of a social insurance nature—say, to fund the recurrent costs of primary health care. IDA funds would thus be used to reduce what is otherwise the high and pro-cyclical volatility of recipient countries' own revenue and (of even more volatile and pro-cyclical) overall donor inflows. Unless and until the IMF can disburse resources in grant form from its Poverty Reduction and Growth Facility, IDA resources should be available, with IMF staff technical input, for this purpose.

For low-income countries, we highlight five specific recommendations for the new president:

1. Signal support for a narrower, more focused range of Bank operations within each low-income country, especially for lending. In the best performing countries, encourage even more budget support, keyed to clear benchmarks on results. In poorly

performing countries, discourage financial support, while increasing administrative budget resources for advisory services, sector work, policy dialogue, and technical assistance.

2. Urge the shareholders to approve a third, grants-only window for countries with very low per capita incomes, for example, below $500.

3. Encourage longer-term commitment periods for the best-performing countries and programs that build in more automatic exit when country performance declines, and propose changes in IDA replenishment arrangements that would reduce disbursement pressures.

4. Work with the IMF and other donors and creditors on an agreed role of the Bank in signaling the adequacy of a country's "development" approach to complement the IMF's macroeconomic signaling.

5. In collaboration with the IMF, develop a facility to make selected IDA countries at very low income levels eligible for automatic additional transfers as grants in the wake of clearly external shocks.

Take Leadership on Ensuring Truly Independent Evaluation of the Impact of Bank and Other Aid-Supported Programs

Agencies that develop and manage development assistance programs hesitate (with some justification) to advertise the limits of their craft. The World Bank is no exception. Although the Bank has improved its transparency through increased in-house research on aid effectiveness and through increasingly frank and systematic work of its internal evaluation department, neither fills the need for credible, fully independent assessment.

This is unfortunate. Rigorous and well-targeted evaluations offer opportunities to substantially expand the impact of Bank-funded efforts beyond any particular country or program. The knowledge they generate is itself a global public good, since the benefit of knowing which programs work and which do not extends well beyond the organization or country implementing a program. Moreover, evaluations of Bank-supported programs that are fully and visibly independent would improve the credibility of the Bank's efforts—and that of other donors—and increase the political support for aid to support demonstrably effective programs. Independent evaluation is particularly critical in the IDA countries, for many of which aid is likely to increase substantially in the next decade.

In 1973 Bank president Robert McNamara created the Operations Evaluation Department (OED), a nominally independent unit within the World Bank reporting directly to the Bank's Board of Executive Directors. OED's primary mission is to conduct ex post assessments of Bank-financed interventions. It does this in two ways: by evaluating projects and by evaluating the Bank's development activities more broadly.[31] In principle, OED reports provide analytical background and support for forward-looking decisionmaking about strategy. In fact, they are by definition untimely because they are conducted ex post (often looking back as much as 10 years). And because they are scrutinized in draft by Bank staff and countries whose programs are the subject of evaluation, there is a natural process of minimizing the harshness of language. In addition, it is difficult for even the best internally sponsored impact evaluations to deal with such fundamental problems as the lack of baseline indicators, controls, and a counterfactual.

To address problems of credibility and independence in evaluation, the Meltzer Commission (International Financial Institution Advisory Commission 2000), the Task Force on the Future of the IMF (ODC 2000), and the Gurría-Volcker Commission (Commission on the Role of the MDBs in Emerging Markets 2001) all recommended the creation of an independent evaluation entity external to the Bank (and the IMF). Gurría-Volcker, for example, calls on shareholders to create a "mechanism for independent, third-party evaluation of the effectiveness for MDB [multilateral development bank] programs [not just the World Bank], and whether such programs... encourage adequate norm-setting, increased attention to poverty reduction, and better policies and stronger institutions generally."[32]

To complicate the challenge, independent evaluation focused solely on Bank-supported projects can only be part of the story. As the Bank and other donors move toward sectorwide and budget support it becomes increasingly difficult to pinpoint a specific project as being funded

Evaluations of Bank-supported programs that are fully and visibly independent would improve the credibility of the Bank's efforts

mainly or entirely by the Bank. But increased country ownership of investment programs does not reduce the need for high quality evaluations. Decisions still need to be made—by governments, local communities, and others in consultation with the Bank and other donors— about the best ways to combat poverty, and the Bank is very well-placed to make an important contribution to the establishment of an evidence base about the effectiveness of alternative strategies through rigorous evaluation. This evidence base can then be drawn upon by all those involved in development to increase the effectiveness of their programs.

The need for impact evaluation of social programs is particularly acute. A forthcoming report of the Center for Global Development will recommend the creation of a voluntary, self-financing consortium of donors, developing countries, foundations, and international NGOs to sponsor and finance independent impact evaluation of selected social programs in low- and middle-income countries. The report recommends that some evaluation resources be earmarked for studies with randomized assignment, which face the largest obstacles relative to their promise in knowledge building.[33]

The new president should lead the creation of an external, independent, multidonor (and creditor) aid evaluation mechanism

The Working Group recommends that the new president lead the creation of an external, independent, multidonor (and creditor) aid evaluation mechanism to:

Take leadership in working with the board to support the creation of an independent evaluation entity financed and governed by a consortium of donors and multinational creditors.

No one member would have control over the entity's operations, but its members would jointly set priorities about evaluation focus areas. The reason behind creating a consortium is that a collective decision, once agreed, would help lock in good behavior of more and better evaluation— insulating specific programs from political pressures associated with negative evaluations.[34] This entity would not focus exclusively on the Bank's activities, or even only on donor-financed activities. It would also assess developing countries' own-financed programs as well as those of NGOs (in all cases based on requests from these entities). The consortium could be financed by contributions from its individual members, ideally linked to each member's own annual aid disbursements.

This entity would assess the effectiveness and impact of the programs and projects supported by the Bank and other creditors and donors, not the policies and processes of the Bank itself (which are already subject to the Inspection Panel). It would complement rather than substitute for the audit and evaluation work of OED (and other internal evaluation offices of other donor and creditor agencies).

The governance of this entity would be determined by its members. Ideally developing country members would join. The Bank's leadership in creating such an entity would thus make at least this aspect of its governance more representative. In any event decisionmaking for Bank programs would continue to rest with the board.[35]

Past investments in global public goods relevant to developing countries have had impressive rates of return

Obtain an Explicit Mandate, an Adequate Grant Instrument, and a Special Governance Structure for the Bank's Work on Global Public Goods

The last 10–15 years have seen increasing attention to international initiatives for the financing and provision of global public goods. Global public goods are those goods (or "bads") that no single nation has a sufficient incentive to produce (or limit) in optimal (from a global standpoint) amounts, but which have benefits (or costs) for all nations. Examples include technological advances in agriculture and health, and global public "bads" such as global warming. Past investments in global public goods relevant to developing countries have had impressive rates of return: as high as 40 percent for agricultural research.[36] The return on a malaria vaccine would be comparable. Investment to reduce or manage expected global warming would have huge benefits (in reduced economic costs) that in welfare terms would be greater for developing than for developed countries.

The Bank has long had some engagement in global public goods, early on primarily through the Consultative Group on International Agricultural Research and then through its role in the Global Environment Facility. Beginning in the early 1990s, it was drawn into financing and providing many other, often smaller programs (for example, support of a consortium of public and private agencies working on microfinance issues). These have generally been housed or run inside the Bank through specific trust funds financed by interested donors—and managed outside the purview of overall Bank budget and program allocations.

The Bank's status as a global institution with a broad and deep range of expertise explains the demands from its shareholders for its technical and financial involvement in a growing range of global programs, some in the category of global public goods (and some basically financing regional and even national programs likely to have some transnational spillovers). It is now involved (either as a member, financier, administrator, or participant) in as many as 70 such programs (table 1). Bank involvement has helped fill the void created in some areas by U.N. agencies and the regional development banks' lack of comparable financial strength or lack of adequate staffing and expertise.

But the result is a peculiar situation of the Bank's having a set of *ad hoc* global programs, sometimes in possible competition with U.N. agencies, without a clear mandate from its shareholders. The shareholders have not considered the need for the Bank to have an instrument comparable to the country loan (with a sovereign guarantee) that would enable it to pursue such a mandate strategically—as opposed to responses to *ad hoc* requests and *ad hoc* special financing. As a result, financing is haphazard. Some programs are financed from the administrative budget, some from transfers from net income, and most from Bank-administered trust funds.[37]

Without its own instrument, it is difficult for the Bank to lead in financing or coordinating consortia to finance new initiatives. As a result, promising programs receive inadequate attention. A good example is a recent detailed proposal for an advance commitment to purchase vaccines for diseases concentrated in low-income countries. The idea of an advance commitment is to provide incentives for private firms to undertake the research and development (R&D) investments needed to develop these vaccines. In addition, the proposed purchase is structured to ensure access to these vaccines for the people who need them most, if and when they are developed. If no vaccine is developed, no Bank or other donor funds would be spent. But if successful, millions of lives would be saved at very low cost (for a malaria vaccine, an estimated $15 per year of life saved).[38]

The Working Group concluded that beyond the widely acknowledged objective of reducing world poverty by supporting equitable growth, there is a case for explicitly extending the Bank's mandate for the financing and provision of global public goods, notably in agriculture, health, and the environment. Already the Bank, as a key player in the management of globalization, is seen as a "go to" institution. But the accretion of responsibilities without a mandate and clarity on financing and instruments has limited its role and risks ineffective use of its global resources. We therefore recommend that the new president:

The new president should call on the Bank's shareholders to give it a clear mandate for financing and providing global public goods

1. Call on the Bank's shareholders to give it a clear mandate for financing and providing global public goods. (We refer here not to any and all forms of global programs but to those that, because of their public good nature, have the least call on country-based financing). Among other benefits, this would give the Bank clear responsibility for clarifying its contribution in the light of broader global priorities for investment in global public goods.

2. Initiate a dialogue with the regional development banks, the United Nations, and other relevant agencies on the proper division of labor between global and regional public goods. In particular, the Bank should avoid involvement in the latter wherever engagement by the regional banks makes sense. Between the banks and the United Nations, there is no obvious right institutional arrangement that would create accountability for the financing and implementation of programs—accountability has to be based on agreements for respective roles.

3. Ask the board's members to create a Global Public Goods Trust Fund managed by the Bank, to consolidate and help set priorities for current spending from the Bank's resources, and to contribute to the financing of such new and promising initiatives as the advance market commitment for vaccines.

4. Encourage agreement on financing the Global Public Goods Trust Fund along the following lines:

- Some portion of the Bank's annual net income should be earmarked for a Global Public Goods Trust Fund. The Bank's net income belongs to all its members, so its benefits should also extend to all its members.
- The donor countries that currently make contributions to the variety of global programs at the Bank should be urged to contribute instead to a single Global Public Goods Trust Fund— where they can with other Bank shareholders, ensure that priorities for Bank work are aligned with resources, and take into account U.N. and regional bank activities.
- A leaner Bank (thanks to a marked reduction in the "hassle" factor and to more automatic and less conditional loans for select eligible borrowers) could reduce administrative costs. The savings could be added to "allocable" net income and used to supplement the financing of global public goods. Similarly, more innovative financial products will induce greater borrowing, which could increase the net income available for global public goods.

Some portion of the Bank's annual net income should be earmarked for a Global Public Goods Trust Fund

We estimate that it should be possible, with these changes, to generate $300–500 million annually for the Global Public Goods Trust Fund.

5. Encourage agreement on a new approach to the governance of the Global Public Goods Trust Fund. Decisions on the use of the trust fund could be made by the board, but with a different allocation of votes (akin to the Global Environment Facility, which also has a different governance structure from the Bank's board). IBRD borrowers ought to control at least 40 percent and IDA-only countries another 10–20 percent. Using net income for global public goods will be seen by middle-income borrowers as imposing the costs on them, since their average borrowing rates would be higher. In particular, to acknowledge their indirect financing role, the middle-income countries and emerging market economies should have a seat

at the table, with considerable input on decisions on which global public goods are to be financed.

6. The trust fund rules should clarify that Bank management need not always be involved in managing the global public goods that the trust fund helps finance.

Push the Bank's Member Governments to Make the Bank's Governance More Representative and Thus More Legitimate

No issue fundamentally affects the legitimacy of the Bank—and its effectiveness—as much as its governance structure

No issue fundamentally affects the legitimacy of the Bank—and its effectiveness—as much as its governance structure. Yet no issue has been as impervious to change. The Bank should become something closer to the spirit of a global "club" in which today's beneficiaries, not only its rich-country benefactors, have a keen sense of ownership and financial responsibility.

Votes

Like most major Fortune 500 companies, each of the agencies that make up the World Bank Group (IBRD, IDA, IFC, and MIGA) has shareholders that own a stake in the organization. The one difference, of course, is that the Bank's shareholders (unlike most multinational corporations) are countries rather than individuals. Each country has a given number of votes linked to the size of its shareholding.

But the size of country shareholdings no longer reflects an appropriate balance between borrowers and nonborrowers. In 1950, for example, when the countries of Western Europe were the major borrowers and beneficiaries of the below-market access to capital the Bank provided, they had some considerable influence on the Bank's policies and practices—through management and staffing as well as their voting shares. Today, however, the Bank's borrowers have virtually no real control over fundamental decisions. For example, Sub-Saharan African countries represent 27 percent of all IDA member countries, but have only 8 percent of the voting shares. Their ownership stake is small, though they are particularly dependent on the Bank, accounting for 20 percent of total Bank lending (IDA plus IBRD) in fiscal 2004.[39]

Part of the difficulty has to do with the lack of consensus on when and whether to alter capital shares. Past changes have come at the time of capital replenishments, when the pie was increasing and countries could buy more shares and increase their percentage of the total. Still, fast-growing China, now constituting an estimated 13 percent of the world economy, holds just 2.8 percent of shares, and India, now 6 percent of the world economy and also growing fast, just 2.8 percent.[40] Meanwhile Saudi Arabia, with 0.6 percent of the world economy, has 2.8 percent of voting shares (and 1 of the 24 board seats). Canada and Italy have the same voting shares as China, and Belgium has 50 percent more votes than Mexico. In a global club, in any event, other factors, including population, might ideally affect voting shares (table 2).[41]

There is a logic in the continuing power and influence of nonborrowers. It ensured the Bank's effectiveness for many years and it helps sustain their support—in

Table 2
Current and Potential Allocation of IBRD Voting Power

	IBRD voting share (% of total)	0.5 (share of population)+ 0.5 (share of world GDP) (%)		IBRD voting share minus	IBRD voting (constant 1995$	GDP GDP (PPP$
		Constant 1995$ GDP	PPP GDP	PPP GDP voting share[a]	billions)	billions)
United States	16.4	15.6	12.9	3.5	9,196	10,357
Japan	7.9	9.3	4.5	3.3	5,725	3,423
Germany	4.5	4.6	3.0	1.5	2,708	2,251
France	4.3	3.1	2.1	2.2	1,832	1,604
United Kingdom	4.3	2.4	2.1	2.2	1,361	1,576
Canada	2.8	1.3	1.2	1.5	741	960
China	2.8	12.1	16.4	−13.6	1,209	5,917
India	2.8	9.2	11.3	−8.5	517	2,769
Italy	2.8	2.2	2.0	0.8	1,234	1,529
Russia	2.8	1.8	2.4	0.4	469	1,207
Saudi Arabia	2.8	0.4	0.5	2.3	166	273
Netherlands	2.2	0.9	0.6	1.6	505	457
Brazil	2.1	2.6	2.8	−0.7	810	1,352
Belgium	1.8	0.5	0.4	1.4	321	286
Spain	1.8	1.4	1.2	0.5	739	886
Switzerland	1.7	0.5	0.3	1.4	339	218
Australia	1.5	0.9	0.7	0.8	481	541
Iran	1.5	0.7	1.0	0.5	118	438
Venezuela	1.3	0.3	0.3	0.9	75	134
Mexico	1.2	1.4	1.8	−0.6	375	915

IBRD is International Bank for Reconstruction and Development.

a. A positive value indicates that the current IBRD voting share is too large given population and PPP GDP; a negative value indicates that a country's IBRD voting share is too small adjusting for population and PPP GDP.

Source: World Bank (2005); IMF (2005b); and author's calculations.

contrast to their less constant support for many of the U.N. agencies and the problems of decisionmaking where the norm is one-country one-vote. Yet in this new century, more accountable and representative institutions within countries are seen as more conducive to poverty-reducing growth, and democracy is broadly acknowledged as the most legitimate form of government. In this context, the continuing lack of influence of borrowers reduces the legitimacy of Bank-supported policies and programs in some borrowing countries. And over the next decade it is likely to further undermine the Bank's effectiveness—including, ironically, the support for better governance in borrowing countries.

The continuing lack of influence of borrowers is likely to further undermine the Bank's effectiveness

Voice

The governance deficit is compounded by the inadequate representation of borrowing countries on the Bank's board. Of the 24 board seats, borrowing countries hold only 9; they share with nonborrowers another 8 (table 3). The limited representation of developing country borrowers on the Bank's board discourages borrowing country board members from any real scrutiny of other borrowers' programs. It also creates time and work pressures that

Table 3 Distribution of Voting Power at the Multilateral Development Banks

	Voting share (%)				Directors					
	United States	Other G-7	Other nonborrower	Developing country borrowers	United States	Other G-7	Other nonborrower	Developing country borrowers	Total	President
International Monetary Fund	17	28	17	38	1	6	6	11	24	Nonborrower
World Bank	16	27	18	39	1	6	8	9	24	Nonborrower
Inter-American Development Bank	30	16	4	50	1	4	0	9	14	Borrower
Asian Development Bank	13	27	15	45	1	4	1	6	12	Nonborrower
African Development Bank	7	21	12	60	1	4	1	12	18	Borrower
European Bank for Reconstruction and Development	10	47	30	13	1	6	12	4	23	Nonborrower

Source: Birdsall 2003.

make it difficult for them to focus on institutional issues while also representing their country interests.

The lack of voice in board representation is acute for the Sub-Saharan countries, which rely heavily on the Bank's advice and financial support. At present, 46 Sub-Saharan countries are represented by just two chairs on the Bank's board, creating a tremendous administrative and procedural burden for the directors and their staffs.

Presidential selection
The president of the Bank is an American, while the managing director of the IMF is European, under an implicit post–World War II agreement. This gives the U.S. administration unchecked discretion in the timing and process for selecting presidents, undermining the sense of ownership that ideally would be shared by more member governments in an institution at the center of a shared global goal to reduce poverty. The point, however, is not fundamentally about nationality. It is that the selection process should be transparent (similar to what the Bank advocates regarding countries' governance), and that it should draw from the global talent pool.[42]

Role of the board
Another governance problem is the board's difficulty in playing a "strategic" role and its inability to make management accountable to it. For many years, close observers of the Bank have questioned the effectiveness of the resident Board, whose members spend full-time on Bank work and may not have the seniority in their governments to influence Bank management priorities.

We recommend that the new president engage early and in open discussion with the Bank governors on how to address these deficits. If politically difficult adjustments are to be made, they will almost surely need to be proposed by the Bank's president. Despite broad support from all shareholders for the principle of better representation, none—and least the most powerful—has any incentive to make a first move. The result is a deep problem of collective gridlock. Because the changes will be difficult, it seems appropriate for the president to open the discussion during his honeymoon, his first months in office.

We recommend that the new president take four specific initiatives to re-establish the legitimacy of the Bank's governance:

Ask for an independent assessment, to be made public, of voting shares and board representation, including options for changes.

1. Ask the governors of the Bank to formalize a credible, rule-based, transparent mechanism (as with private sector boards) for choosing the Bank's president. A 2001 joint report to the Bank and IMF boards, originated by working groups set up by each institution, outlined one possible mechanism.[43] The report was endorsed by both boards as guidance for future selection processes.[44] In broad terms, the report advocated the creation of an advisory group that would assist the executive directors in presidential selection by developing a slate of candidates and providing assessments of each candidate to the executive directors, who would maintain responsibility for approving a presidential candidate.

2. Support the temporary establishment (say, for a decade) of two additional seats on the board for African countries.[45] (In the longer term, if the Board is to be more strategic, there is a good case for reducing its size, which could be achieved, for example, with a decline in the representation of Europe, the most overrepresented region, and merging the Saudi seat with that representing other Arab nations).

3. Ask the Bank governors to call for an independent assessment, to be made public, of voting shares and board representation, including options for changes. Options should explore among other issues increases in the basic votes, the merits of applying double majorities on some decisions (that is, 50 percent of all votes plus 50 percent of all members), and should take into account discussions at the IMF of its quota distribution during its current quota review period. The recent communiqué of the International Monetary and Financial Committee of the IMF on quota reallocations stated that "adequate voice and participation by all members should be assured, and the distribution of quotas should reflect developments in the world economy."[46] Desirable changes at the IMF and World Bank would only reinforce what has already been acknowledged by the creation in 1999 of the Group of 20 (a new club consisting of the G-8 and such major emerging market countries as Brazil, China, and India) to deal with key issues in the international monetary and financial system.[47]

4. Ask the governors to commission a time-bound independent review of board functions and responsibilities. A review of the board should examine how to make the board more strategic, with emphasis on its central task of setting objectives and holding management to account. It could also address how to trim back the board's ballooning budget, which sends the wrong signals on corporate governance. Meanwhile, push for such interim steps as holding occasional board meetings in borrowing countries—to help focus the board on strategic issues in a particular region and to foster greater ownership among borrowers. A board meeting in Pretoria, for instance, would highlight the strategic issues of concern to Southern Africa and make it possible to invite particular borrowing countries to play a more central role in the board meeting, perhaps by giving brief presentations on issues of particular relevance.

Almost every new regime enjoys a brief honeymoon to put taboo issues on the table for debate and discussion

We would like to emphasize that the new president's agenda on reforming the Bank's governance structure is for the medium term. Transforming the Bank from a traditional development agency to a "club" where both donors and borrowers have equal ownership and responsibility will take time, but many Working Group members considered it the single biggest challenge facing the new president. Almost every new regime enjoys a brief honeymoon to put taboo issues on the table for debate and discussion. A strong statement early on could help set the tone of the governance debate and give the issue some much-needed momentum.

* * * * *

One temptation the new president should eschew is an immediate and far-reaching administrative reorganization. In the past these have been hugely expensive and disruptive, with little to show for all the smoke and fire. Instead, we propose two modest changes that would considerably improve the administrative efficiency of the Bank. One: simplify regulations to ease out underperforming staff. For all its bravado about the need for labor market flexibility in its borrowers, the Bank has been loath to follow its own advice resulting in bloated costs and lower efficiency. Two: strengthen internal incentives for staff to work in the poorest and weakest countries. That would change a common perception that Bank employees should have significant experience on the larger, middle-income countries if they are to be considered qualified candidates for senior positions within Bank management.

Biographies of Working Group Members

K. Y. Amoako
K. Y. Amoako is executive secretary of the Economic Commission for Africa (UNECA), the regional arm of the United Nations in Africa, serving at the rank of under-secretary-general of the United Nations. He is also a member of U.K. Prime Minister Tony Blair's Commission for Africa. Prior to joining UNECA in 1995, he served at the World Bank for two decades and worked in many areas of the Bank's activities, including country operations, sector operations, sector policy, and personnel management. He also held senior positions, including director of the Education and Social Policy Department (1993–95).

Owen Barder
Owen Barder is a senior program associate at the Center for Global Development, where he works on communications and outreach activities primarily associated with the Policy Research Network on Global Public Health. Most recently, he served as the director of Information, Communications, and Knowledge and head of Africa policy for the U.K. Department for International Development. He has also served as private secretary to the Prime Minister (Economic Affairs) and in the U.K. Treasury, where he was seconded to the South African Treasury.

Nancy Birdsall
Nancy Birdsall is the founding president of the Center for Global Development. Before launching the Center, she served for three years as senior associate and director of the Economic Reform Project at the Carnegie Endowment for International Peace. From 1993 to 1998, she was executive vice president of the Inter-American Development Bank. Before that she spent 14 years in research, policy, and management positions at the World Bank. She is the author, coauthor, or editor of more than a dozen books and monographs on international development issues.

Colin I. Bradford

Colin Bradford is a visiting fellow in economic studies at the Brookings Institution. He currently serves as adviser to the Global Economy Track of the Helsinki Process on Globalization and Democracy. Previously, he was research professor of economics and international relations at American University and chief economist of the U.S. Agency for International Development. He also has held senior positions at the Organisation for Economic Co-operation and Development, the World Bank, and the Yale University School of Organization and Management.

Ariel Buira

Ariel Buira is currently director of the G-24 Secretariat. He is a former staff member and executive director of the International Monetary Fund. He has been international director and member of the Board of Governors of Banco de Mexico, ambassador of Mexico to Greece, special envoy of the president of Mexico for the U.N. Conference on Financing for Development, and senior member of Saint Antony's College, Oxford. His latest publications include *Challenges to the World Bank and the IMF* (Anthem Press, 2003) and *The IMF and the World Bank at Sixty* (Anthem Press, 2005).

Kenneth W. Dam

Ken Dam is Max Pam Professor Emeritus of American & Foreign Law and Senior Lecturer at the University of Chicago Law School and senior fellow in Economic Studies at the Brookings Institution. He has had a distinguished career in public service, including as deputy secretary in the U.S. Departments of Treasury and State, executive director of the Council on Economic Policy, and assistant director in the Office of Management and Budget. He has also held positions as vice president for law and external relations at IBM and as president and chief executive officer of the United Way of America.

Robert E. Evenson

Robert Evenson is professor of economics and director of the International and Development Economics Program at Yale University. He joined the Yale faculty in 1969 and is the author or co-author of hundreds of scientific papers on agricultural productivity and economic growth in low-income countries. From 1997 to 2000 he was director of the Economic Growth Center at Yale University. His most recent book is *Crop Variety Improvement and Its Effect on Productivity: The Impact of International Agricultural Research* (2003).

Jo Marie Griesgraber

Jo Marie Griesgraber is the director of the New Rules for Global Finance, a coalition of nongovernmental organizations and scholars dedicated to the reform of the global financial architecture. She also serves as vice-president and secretary of the Financial Policy Forum. Previously she served as the policy director for Oxfam America, the director of Rethinking Bretton Woods project at the Center for Concern, and the deputy director of the Washington Office on Latin America.

José Angel Gurría

José Angel Gurría is the former minister of foreign affairs (1994–97) and former minister of finance (1998–2000) of Mexico and was a Mexican civil servant for 33 years. He headed Mexico's foreign financing strategy in the late 1970s and early 1980s and Mexico's debt restructuring negotiations during the late 1980s and early 1990s. He co-chaired (with Paul Volcker) the Commission on the Role of the MDBs in Emerging Markets in 2001 and chaired the External Advisory Group on the future of the Inter-American Development Bank. He is presently a member of the board of a number of nonprofit institutions, including the Center for Global Development, the Population Council, and the U.N. Secretary General's Advisory Board on Water. He is also a member of a number of advisory boards and boards of directors for private companies in Mexico, Spain, and the United States.

Pierre Jacquet

Pierre Jacquet has been executive director (in charge of strategy) and chief economist at Agence Française de Développement (the French Development Agency) since 2002. He was formerly deputy director of the French Institute of International Relations in Paris and chief editor of its quarterly review *Politique Etrangère.* He is professor of international economics and chairman of the Department of Economics and Social Aciences at Ecole Nationale des Ponts et Chaussées. He is also a member of the Conseil d'Analyse Economique, an independent advisory panel created by the French Prime Minister in July 1997.

Edward V.K. ("Kim") Jaycox

Kim Jaycox is a managing director of EMP Global, a Washington-based manager of private equity funds operating in emerging markets. He is also the CEO of the AIG African Infrastructure Fund. He served at the World Bank for over 30 years, including as vice president in charge of the Bank's operations in Sub-Saharan Africa from 1984 to 1996. Previously, he directed the World Bank's programs in East Asia and led the team that brought the People's Republic of China into the Bank.

Devesh Kapur

Devesh Kapur is an associate professor in the Department of Government at Harvard University. He serves concurrently as director of the Graduate Student Associate Program and faculty associate at the Weatherhead Center for International Affairs and the Center for International Development at the John F. Kennedy School of Government at Harvard University. He is also a non-resident fellow at the Center for Global Development. He is the author of *Give Us Your Best and Brightest* (Center for Global Development, forthcoming) and co-author of *The World Bank: Its First Half Century* (Brookings Institution, 1997).

Michael Kremer

Michael Kremer is Gates Professor of Developing Societies at Harvard University, senior fellow at the Brookings Institution, and a non-resident fellow at the Center for Global Development. He is research associate at the National Bureau of Economic Research; vice-president of the Bureau for Research and Economic Analysis of Development; and a fellow of the Academy of Arts and Sciences. He serves as associate editor of the *Journal of Development Economics* and the *Quarterly Journal of Economics*. He is author, most recently, of *Strong Medicine: Creating Incentives for Pharmaceutical Research on Neglected Diseases* (Princeton, 2004).

Steven Radelet

Steven Radelet is a senior fellow at the Center for Global Development, where he works on issues related to foreign aid, developing country debt, economic growth, and trade between rich and poor countries. He was deputy assistant secretary of the U.S. Treasury for Africa, the Middle East, and Asia from January 2000 through June 2002. From 1990 to 2000, he was on the faculty of Harvard University, where he was a fellow at the Harvard Institute for International Development, director of its Macroeconomics Program, and a lecturer on economics and public policy. He is the author of *Challenging Foreign Aid: A Policymaker's Guide to the Millennium Challenge Account* (CGD, 2003).

Jean-Michel Severino

Jean-Michel Severino was appointed director general of Agence Française de Développement (the French Development Agency) in 2001. He was previously vice-president for the Asia region in the World Bank, which he joined in 1996. Prior to joining the World Bank, he spent eight years in various positions at the French Ministry for Co-operation and Development and served as inspector of finance in the French Ministry of Economy and Finance. He was nominated general-inspector of finance and associate professor at the CERDI–University of Auvergne in 2000.

Vito Tanzi

Vito Tanzi is a consultant at the Inter-American Development Bank. He spent more than 25 years at the International Monetary Fund, including as chief of the Tax Policy Division and director of the Fiscal Affairs Department. In addition, he has served as undersecretary in Italy's Ministry of Economy and Finance, senior associate at the Carnegie Endowment for International Peace, president of the International Institute of Public Finance, and chairman of the Economics Department at American University in Washington, D.C.

Daniel K. Tarullo

Daniel K. Tarullo is professor of law at Georgetown University Law Center. From 1993 to 1998 he was, successively, assistant secretary of state for economic and business affairs, deputy assistant to the president for economic policy, and assistant to the president for international economic policy. From 1995 to 1998 he was also President Bill Clinton's personal representative to the G-7/G-8 group of industrialized nations. Prior to joining the Clinton administration, he practiced law for several years in Washington, D.C., mostly in the areas of antitrust, financial markets, and international transactions. Previously, he was chief counsel on the staff of Senator Edward M. Kennedy.

John Williamson

John Williamson has been a senior fellow at the Institute of International Economics since 1981. He was project director for the U.N. High-Level Panel on Financing for Development (the Zedillo Report) in 2001 and on leave as chief economist for South Asia at the World Bank during 1996–99. He has held faculty positions at Pontificia Universidade Católica do Rio de Janeiro, University of Warwick, Massachusetts Institute of Technology, University of York, and Princeton University. He is author or editor of numerous studies on international monetary and developing-world debt issues, including *Delivering on Debt Relief: From IMF Gold to a New Aid Architecture* (Center for Global Development and Institute for International Economics, 2002).

Ngaire Woods

Ngaire Woods is director of the Global Economic Governance Programme at University College, Oxford. She is an adviser to the United Nations Development Programme's Human Development Report Office, a member of the Helsinki Process on global governance, and a member of the resource group of the U.N. Secretary-General's High-Level Commission into Threats, Challenges and Change. She sits on numerous editorial and advisory boards, including the Advisory Group of the Center for Global Development. Her most recent book is *Global Mission: the IMF, the World Bank and Their Borrowers* (Cornell University Press, forthcoming).

Daniel M. Zelikow

Daniel M. Zelikow is a managing director of JP Morgan and a member of the Government Institutions Group with responsibility for multilateral financial institutions, export credit agencies, and some of JPMorgan's key emerging markets clients. He also coordinates JP Morgan's activities to facilitate Iraq's financial reconstruction and helped to found the Trade Bank of Iraq. Before joining JPMorgan in 1999, he served as deputy assistant secretary for international affairs at the U.S. Treasury. Before managing the U.S. financial support program for Mexico in 1995 as head of the Mexico Task Force, he directed the Treasury's overseas technical cooperation, involving finance ministries and central banks in more than 20 countries.

Notes

1. Einhorn (2001).
2. For a critique from the left, see 50 Years Is Enough (2004). For a conservative critique, see International Financial Institution Advisory Commission (2000). For a useful summary of critiques emanating from both sides, see Mallaby (2005).
3. See Einhorn (2001).
4. According to an internal Bank audit, "The Bank faces challenges in effectively customizing its...poverty reduction strategy to individual countries. The Bank needs to apply its strategy based on detailed country knowledge and an appreciation of the willingness and ability of each country to implement reforms." See World Bank, Operations Evaluation Department (2005).
5. For an illustration of this renewed emphasis on infrastructure, see the final report on IDA-14 replenishment (IDA 2005).
6. World Bank, Operations Evaluation Department (2005) suggests the Bank has encouraged too much lending for social programs in low-income countries, neglecting the role of infrastructure in growth. It does not make the point that even among the low-income group, decisions across programs (agriculture, social, infrastructure, civil service reform, and more) need to be made on a country-by-country basis.
7. The Working Group did not discuss the management question of how much more Bank staff should be decentralized to work outside of Washington, beyond the observation that the direction of the last decade toward greater decentralization has made the Bank more effective.
8. According to World Bank, Operations Evaluation Department (2005), the Bank must undertake a "realistic assessment of the political environment and the implementation capacity for reform" if it is to strike the optimal balance between economic growth and long-term institutional and social development objectives.
9. In turn this requires that the Bank be much more aware that most of its knowledge generation is for all practical purposes unavailable to the very audience

whose problems it is designed to address—poor and marginalized communities—because it is rarely in the languages of these communities. One highly cost-effective way to increase the impact of the Bank's expertise is to make the Bank's Web site multilingual in the languages most widely used in client countries. Surveys show strong demand for this service; yet most of the Bank's knowledge is available only in English. See World Bank (2004b).

10. The majority's vision was that, "all resource transfers to countries that enjoy capital-market access (as denoted by an investment-grade international bond rating) or with a per capita income in excess of $4,000 would be phased out over the next 5 years." See International Financial Institution Advisory Commission (2000), p. 82. That position had earlier been stated, and has since been restated and extended, by such distinguished economists as Kenneth Rogoff, the former director of research of the IMF, who remarked in a recent public forum that it makes little sense for the World Bank to be lending to China, with its high levels of foreign direct investment and growing dollar reserves, which are the source of huge flows to the United States.

11. See Commission on the Role of the MDBs in Emerging Markets (2001). This Commission is often referred to as the "Gurría-Volcker Commission" after its chairs, José Angel Gurría and Paul Volcker.

12. The Working Group concluded, in contrast, that the World Bank should continue to be active in middle-income countries and in such emerging markets as China and India. Working Group member Daniel Tarullo would be very cautious about the nature of World Bank involvement in middle-income and other countries with significant, sustained inflows of capital.

13. What they lack is long-date, fixed-rate access in local currency because of investors' concerns about their macroeconomic stability.

14. See Commission on the Role of the MDBs in Emerging Markets (2001), from which some of the text on this issue is excerpted.

15. To the extent that countries rely solely on access to private markets (including their own internal markets) for these investments they are likely to end up with a dangerous mismatch between short-term liabilities and long-term returns—thus the problem of vulnerability to external capital markets.

16. Based on Nancy Birdsall and Javed Burki's personal discussions and correspondence in 2000–01 with officials of Brazil, Chile, China, Hungary, India, Mexico, and Poland as background work for the Gurría-Volcker Commission. See Commission on the Role of the MDBs in Emerging Markets (2001). Rodrik (1995) emphasizes that for private markets, the credibility of the signaling function of the World Bank and other official creditors rests on the latter's view that "in the absence of direct lending, there is very little to ensure that the official creditors will exercise their informational function as competently as possible.

17. The objective in principle is for the Bank to cover non-commercial risk.

18. The Bank might also help out with some risks for which there is no market (certain commodities, drought) by owning them directly as an insurer.

19. For one perspective on the proliferation of standards and their unintended consequences, see chapter 10 of Mallaby (2004). See also World Bank (2001a, 2001b).

20. This solution was first put forward by Eichengreen and Hausmann (2003).

21. This approach is proposed in Dervis (2005).

22. This uses the market as a benchmark, with richer borrowers paying a rate closer to the market rate they face.

23. One way to do this would be for the Bank to do more blending of its loans with bilateral grants of donors into single coordinated operations.

24. See World Bank (forthcoming). For an exposition specific to Latin America, see Birdsall and de la Torre (2001).

25. Regarding the Poverty Reduction Strategy Papers, see World Bank, Operations Evaluation Department (2004). Regarding reluctance to exit and other failings of donors in low-income countries, see Nancy Birdsall, "Seven Deadly Sins: Reflections on Donor Failings," Center for Global Development Working Paper Number 50, December 2004.

26. This is the spirit behind the Bank's Comprehensive Development Framework, which by its own description "emphasizes the interdependence of all elements of development—social, structural, human, governance, environmental, economic, and financial." For more information on the Comprehensive Development Framework, see http://www.worldbank.org/cdf.

27. See Radelet (2004).

28. Working in these countries is much riskier than other places. As a result, programs in poorly governed states require very careful monitoring, regular re-appraisal, flexible responses as initiatives begin to work or fail, and a higher tolerance for failure than when working in other countries.

29. The exact amount would ideally be specified in purchasing power parity (PPP) terms and in those terms would probably be higher, as only a handful of countries are now at an estimated $500 per capita income or less in PPP terms. In usual exchange rate terms the amount would ideally be smaller: about 40 countries, including fast-growing Vietnam, have incomes per capita below $500 in those terms. On the idea of a second IDA window, see Radelet (forthcoming).

30. Whether the current three-year cycle of IDA replenishments affects that ability is not clear. A longer replenishment period should not be necessary, as IDA already makes commitments beyond three years. But it might help, particularly since bilateral aid commitments over long periods are even more difficult to make.

31. In addition to OED, the Bank created the Inspection Panel in 1993, a three-member body charged with providing an independent forum to private citizens who believe that they or their interests have been or could be directly harmed by a Bank-financed project. The Bank's Executive Board reviews the Panel's recommendations and decides whether an investigation should take place.

32. In the words of the Meltzer Commission (International Financial Institution Advisory Commission 2000), "The project evaluation process at the World Bank gets low marks for credibility: wrong criteria combine with poor timing...The Bank measures results at the moment of final disbursement of funds. Final disbursement often occurs more than one year before the project begins full operations. The start of operations is too early to judge sustainability of achievements... Evaluation should be a repetitive process spread over time including many years after final disbursement of funds, when an operational history is available" (p. 75). See also Commission on the Role of the MDBs in Emerging Markets (2001).

33. See Center for Global Development (forthcoming).

34. Birdsall (2004).

35. Center for Global Development (forthcoming).

36. See Evenson (2003).

37. In fiscal year 2001 (the most recent year for which data are available), the Bank spent about $30 million of its administrative budget on global programs, provided another $120 million in grants (also from its administrative budget under the umbrella of the "Development Grant Facility") and disbursed $500 million from Bank-administered trust funds financed by other contributors. See World Bank, Operations Evaluation Department (2002).

38. The U.K. government has proposed supporting, in collaboration with other donors, such commitments for malaria and HIV vaccines, and we recommend that the Bank take a leadership role in supporting this initiative. The best option would be for the Bank to legally bind itself to provide IDA loans to any IDA-eligible member that wanted to purchase the vaccine as long as a number of pre-specified vaccine characteristics were met. For more detail on advance purchase commitments, see Center for Global Development (2005).

39. See World Bank (2004a). The World Bank's Articles of Agreement do not allow split voting; all of the votes of a given "chair" are cast as a unit. As a result, developing country members of mixed constituencies (for example, the chairs held by the Netherlands, Belgium, Switzerland, and Canada) often go unheard on policy matters when their interests differ from those of the industrial country that represents them as the chair.

40. Data in this paragraph refer to IBRD voting shares. Calculations of the shares of world GDP are in purchasing power parity terms, and data are from the IMF (2005a).

41. Dervis (2005) proposes inclusion of population and of contributions to the United Nations in his formula for representation on the U.N. Security Council.

42. The need for transparency in the selection process was noted by outgoing President James Wolfensohn at his farewell news conference on May 4, 2005. He referred to the World Trade Organization model, which recently chose its new director general from four public candidates. The recent appointment of a new administrator of the United Nations Development Programme was also made following an open selection process, with six candidates.

43. See World Bank and IMF (2001).

44. However, neither board formally adopted the specific recommendations contained in the report.

45. This echoes a similar recommendation made by the U.K.-sponsored Commission for Africa (2005), which advocates for two new African chairs on the Boards of the World Bank and IMF: "As the rules for representation on the Boards [of the World Bank and IMF] are based on economic criteria, it is not likely that African representation will exceed two chairs out of 24 in the short term. However, a decision could be taken by consensus to allow the creation, on a temporary basis (for the entire period up to 2015), of two supplementary positions of Executive Director for Africa, each backed by an Alternate Director, in each Board. This would ease the task of the directors in this critical period for Africa's development" (p. 368).

46. The communiqué states: "The IMF's effectiveness and credibility as a cooperative institution must be safeguarded and further enhanced. Adequate voice and participation by all members should be assured, and the distribution of quotas should reflect developments in the world economy. The Committee emphasizes that the period of the Thirteenth General Review of Quotas provides an opportunity for the membership to make progress toward a consensus on the issues of quotas, voice, and participation" (IMF 2005b).

47. See also Dervis (2005).

References

50 Years Is Enough. 2004. "10 Things You Really Should Know about the World Bank." Washington, D.C.

Birdsall, Nancy. 2003. "Why It Matters Who Runs the IMF and the World Bank." Working Paper 22. Center for Global Development, Washington, D.C. Also in Josack, S., G. Ranis, and J. Vreeland, eds. Forthcoming. *Globalization and the Nation State: The Impact of the IMF and the World Bank.* London: Routledge.

Birdsall, Nancy. 2004. "Seven Deadly Sins: Reflections on Donor Failings." Working Paper 50. Center for Global Development, Washington, D.C.

Birdsall, Nancy, and Augusto de la Torre. 2001. *Washington Contentious: Economic Policies for Social Equity in Latin America*. Washington, D.C.: Carnegie Endowment for International Peace and the Inter-American Dialogue.

Center for Global Development. 2005. *Making Markets for Vaccines: Ideas to Action*. Report of the Advance Market Commitment Working Group. Washington, D.C.

Center for Global Development. Forthcoming. "When Will We Ever Learn? Recommendations to Improve Social Development Assistance through Improved Impact Evaluation." Report of the Development Evaluation Gap Working Group. Washington, D.C.

Commission for Africa. 2005. *Our Common Interest*. London.

Commission on the Role of the MDBs in Emerging Markets. 2001. *The Role of the Multilateral Development Banks in Emerging Market Economies*. Carnegie Endowment for International Peace, EMP Financial Advisors, LLC, and the Inter-American Dialogue, Washington, D.C.

Dervis, Kemal. 2005. A Better Globalization: Legitimacy, Governance, and Reform. Washington, D.C.: Center for Global Development.

Eichengreen, Barry, and Ricardo Hausmann. 2003. "The Road to Redemption." In *Other People's Money: Debt Denomination and Financial Instability in Emerging-Market Economies*. Chicago, Ill.: University of Chicago Press.

Einhorn, Jessica. 2001. "The World Bank's Mission Creep." *Foreign Affairs* 80(5): 22–31.

Evenson, Robert. 2003. "Production Impacts of Crop Genetic Improvement." In R. E. Evenson and D. Gollin, eds., *Crop Variety Improvement and its Effect on Productivity*. Wallingford, U.K.: CABI Publishing.

IDA (International Development Association). 2005. "Additions to IDA Resources: Fourteenth Replenishment—Working Together to Achieve the Millennium Development Goals." Report from the Executive Directors of the International Development Association to the Board of Governors. Washington, D.C.

IMF (International Monetary Fund). 2005a. "Communiqué of the International Monetary and Financial Committee of the Board of Governors of the International Monetary Fund." Press Release 05/87, April 16. Washington, D.C.

————. 2005b. *World Economic Outlook.* Washington, D.C.

International Financial Institution Advisory Commission. 2000. "International Financial Institutions Reform." Washington, D.C.

Mallaby, Sebastian. 2004. *The World's Banker: A Story of Failed States, Financial Crises, and the Wealth and Poverty of Nations.* New York: Penguin Press.

————. 2005. "Saving the World Bank." *Foreign Affairs* 84(3): 75–85.

ODC (Overseas Development Council). 2000. "Report of the Task Force on the Future of the IMF." Washington, D.C.

Radelet, Steven. 2004. "Aid Effectiveness and the Millennium Development Goals." Working Paper 39, Center for Global Development, Washington, D.C.

————. Forthcoming. "Grants or Loans? How Should the World Bank Distribute Funds to the World's Poorest Countries?" Center for Global Development, Washington, D.C.

Rodrik, Dani. 1995. *Why Is There Multilateral Lending?* NBER Working Paper 5160. Cambridge, Mass.: National Bureau of Economic Research.

World Bank. 2001a. "Report of the Task Force on the Cost of Doing Business." Washington, D.C.

————. 2001b. "Report of the Task Force on the World Bank Group and the Middle-Income Countries." Washington, D.C.

————. 2004a. *Annual Report 2004: Volume One.* Washington, D.C.

————. 2004b. "Why The World Bank Needs a Multilingual Web Site and What to Do About It." Washington, D.C.

————. 2005. *World Development Indicators.* Washington, D.C.

————. Forthcoming. *World Development Report 2006: Equity and Development.* Washington, D.C.

World Bank, Operations Evaluation Department. 2002. *The World Bank's Approach to Global Programs—An Independent Evaluation: Phase 1 Report.* Washington, D.C.

————. 2004. *The Poverty Reduction Strategy Initiative: An Independent Evaluation of the World Bank's Support Through 2003*. Washington, D.C.

————. 2005. *2004 Annual Review of Development Effectiveness: The Bank's Contributions to Poverty Reduction*. Washington, D.C.

World Bank and IMF (International Monetary Fund). 2001. "Draft Joint Report of the Bank Working Group to Review the Process for Selection of the President and The Fund Working Group to Review the Process for Selection of the Managing Director." Washington, D.C.

SELECTED
ESSAYS

A Global Credit Club, Not Another Development Agency

by Nancy Birdsall

In 2000 the majority report of the Meltzer Commission[1] called for the World Bank to get out of lending and move to grants and small technical-assistance programs for the poorer countries—to become a "World Development Agency." In one of the essays in this volume, Adam Lerrick makes a similar case—that because private capital is now available to many developing countries, and given that many developing countries are indeed borrowing less from the World Bank, it is time to push the shareholders and management to focus much more on the poorest countries.

In this essay I argue that the last thing the world needs is another development agency. We have a multitude of those—USAID, the British DFID, and the bilateral aid agencies of at least two dozen other advanced economies; UNICEF, UNIFEM, UNDP, and the European Union; the Red Cross, Oxfam, and World Wildlife Fund; and so on.[2] What the world does need is more global clubs of countries—where decisions, as in country-based democracies, are based on shared discourse, and implementation of decisions is effective because the process is viewed as legitimate in reconciling conflicting views. (The word "club" has different connotations in different cultures and settings. I use it in the everyday "American" sense, which implies open membership not exclusivity—for example the local Rotary Club not the country club.)

The World Bank can be thought of as a particular type of global club, with a structure close to that of a credit union in which the members are nations. Its mission is in the common interests of all its country members: broadly shared and sustainable global prosperity.

Nancy Birdsall, Center for Global Development
Nancy Birdsall is the founding president of the Center for Global Development. Before launching the Center, she was the senior associate and director of the Economic Reform Project at the Carnegie Endowment for International Peace. Birdsall was previously executive vice president of the Inter-American Development Bank and director of the World Bank's research department. She is the author, co-author, or editor of more than a dozen books and monographs.

(Economists might think of this mission as one of working for convergence—of accelerating the process by which relatively poorer nations converge, through development and transformation, toward the prosperity of their richer counterparts.)

In the light of this (simple) idea of the Bank as a credit club, I review here the challenges the Bank faces, including those set out in the preceding report as "five crucial tasks" for the Bank's newest president (in the report I co-chaired with Devesh Kapur, hereafter referred to as the "Working Group Report"), and those debated and discussed in the 11 essays that follow.

Bretton Woods: Inventing a global credit club

The World Bank is not of course the only global club (the largest in number of members is obviously the United Nations), and it is not the only credit union whose members are countries—there are, for example, the regional development banks, the European Investment Bank, and for some aspects of development there is the International Monetary Fund. However, it is the only truly global club that has the financial structure of a credit union. Let us call it, informally, a "global credit club."

In this global credit club, different members have different amounts of "deposits" and provide different amounts of guarantees. The biggest depositor is the U.S. government and, along with Europe and Japan, the United States is the World Bank's biggest guarantor. It and its rich country colleagues back all the borrowing of this peculiar credit union, whether the credit union makes good loans or bad loans, and whether its member country borrowers pay up or not (though history indicates that only rarely do they fail to pay on time).[3] The guarantees (and perhaps the extraordinarily low default rate) mean that this credit union, even with relatively low deposits in the form of paid-in capital, can borrow outside at good rates, and lend at good rates to its less wealthy members.

The global credit club was the brilliant invention of U.K. economist John Maynard Keynes, along with the American, Harry Dexter White, and their colleagues from 42 other countries who conceived the Bank and the IMF at the Bretton Woods Conference in 1944. They conceived of a global club which, at low financial cost to the big depositors and guarantors (at that time, only the United States for all practical purposes), would reduce borrowing costs for the poorer members (at that time war-torn Europe) and make the world richer and safer.

The boundaries within which the club would operate were well understood and fully embraced by the club members. This club was established to promote an open and liberal international economic system, based on market-driven growth and trade (in notable contrast to the system espoused by the Soviet Union (then in 1944 a wartime ally). It would do so by helping the war-ravaged countries of Europe and the poorer countries of Asia, Latin America and Africa make the investments that would enable them to prosper as partners in this open system—in the interests of global stability and security.

Note the financing mechanism for this global credit club did not rely on "contributions" to finance "transfers" from rich to poor nations (though later the club members created a separate club for that purpose, called IDA, in which only the rich country contributors have membership rights). Keynes and his colleagues did not invent a development agency, and did not conceive of the resulting financing as a transfer. On the contrary, the borrowers (at that time to be primarily the Western Europeans) were thought of as full members and partners in the club's venture. Today, as is the case with an everyday credit union, the World Bank's capacity to make loans at low costs to borrowers arises because the sum of the membership's credibility reduces borrowing costs for all members below what they would pay on their own. (This would be true even for the rich countries—their cost of borrowing would be reduced slightly because of the lower risk associated with their diversity. Even today, Germany borrows from the European Investment Bank.)

Today: An aid agency?

It is surprising how far the World Bank of today has strayed, in spirit at least, from this original conception. To quote Jessica Einhorn in her recent essay on the World Bank in *Foreign Affairs*: "Over time, the Bank has evolved from an organization focused on growth through trade and investment to an organization set on achieving a world without poverty. *Its core mission is no longer to partner with … countries in their pursuit of balanced and externally oriented growth; it is to alleviate poverty…*" (italics added).[4] And to quote from the Working Group

Report: "The Bank's mission is to reduce poverty in developing countries."[5]

Much of the discussion and debate about the World Bank today—its effectiveness, its relevance, and its legitimacy—is framed by this different way of describing its basic mission. The different conception is not entirely recent. The non-borrowers established the IDA window for lending to the poorest countries on the basis of outright contributions in 1960—creating in effect an "aid agency" inside the existing club. The speech of Robert McNamara, the Bank's fifth president, in Nairobi in 1973 perhaps marks the official birth of the "poverty" mission for the Bank group as a whole, including the IBRD. Up to that time the Bank was primarily a financier of bricks and mortar projects, with investment in infrastructure seen as the key to open, market-based growth. By the time of James Wolfensohn, the poverty objective had matured and was captured aptly in the lobby of the Bank's main building: "Our dream is a world free of poverty," and in a noteworthy increase in the proportion of Bank lending for social programs.

Is there much real difference between a credit club with an objective of shared global prosperity in an open liberal economy, and a development agency to battle poverty, given that market-led growth and poverty reduction are generally mutually reinforcing? The difference is in part between a club with a mission in every member's interest (global security and prosperity in an open system), versus an aid agency in which some parties are "contributing" to further the interests of others. But in terms of what the Bank is meant to do, broadly defined—provide loans to help countries accelerate their growth and development (and reduce poverty)—there is of course no obvious difference.

Where differences do arise, however, is in the specific priorities and choices and the process for making those choices. Thus over the last several decades, the debate about the relative importance of "growth" versus "poverty reduction" at the Bank has been associated with periods of emphasis on lending for infrastructure for "growth," versus health and education for "poverty reduction."[6] Perhaps more in the spirit of an aid agency than a cooperative, the pendulum is now swinging back to "infrastructure," but with the explicit objective of "poverty reduction"! Similarly, recently the pendulum has swung away from "conditionality" (a process associated with the Bank and often its powerful non-borrowers insisting on their view of what policies would generate development) to the more club-like spirit embodied in the emphasis on "ownership" by member borrowers of their own reforms, and on the importance of "participation" within developing countries of citizens in deciding on reforms.[7]

Three problems, five tasks

The fact is that the distinction between club and aid agency, subtle as it may be, matters for the future of the World Bank. The Bank is under tremendous pressure today. It is assailed from the left for lack of *legitimacy*—for promoting privileged "insider" financial and corporate interests instead of addressing the needs of the voiceless poor. It is assailed from the right for its refusal to admit to its lost *relevance*; with increasing flows of private capital to the developing world (and ample reserves in China, India and many other emerging markets), why use public resources to subsidize loans to those settings—where private markets and private transfers would be more efficient and effective?[8] In the center, from inside as well as outside the Bank, it is criticized for lack of *effectiveness* in attacking poverty in the poorest countries, for its lack of agility in responding to the real demands of its large- and middle-income borrowers (and thus its apparent loss of relevance), and for its loss of institutional focus, as it responds to ever-expanding demands on it from (ironically some would say) its more powerful members: to do everything from assessing needs in Gaza and Iraq, to managing a global program to "fast-track" education gains, to piloting trading across countries in carbon emissions rights.

The pressures have to do with three problems—erosion of the Bank's legitimacy as an institution, loss of faith in its effectiveness (in reducing poverty and in promoting "balanced and externally oriented growth"), and its apparent growing irrelevance. It is these problems in their various forms that authors of the preceding Working Group Report and the essays that follow—all supporters of the Bank's fundamental mission and of its continued existence in some form—address, with proposals for change and reform.

How might the Bank's shareholders, especially the United States, by embracing a vision of the Bank as a club (rather than as a development agency) be better positioned to address these problems? How might a return to the spirit of Bretton Woods, to the idea of a global credit club, change the outlines of the current debates among the Bank's critics about the institution? How might that conception shape changes in the policies and practices of the Bank, including along the lines of the proposed "five crucial tasks" set out in the report above? I address the "club" question now in the context of the five issues or tasks set out in that report.

1. Governance: Does the Bank have legitimacy?

How did the founders make operational the idea of a global credit club? They agreed that in this club, voting power would be related to members' "dues" (or deposits and guarantees), and the deposits and guarantees would be broadly related to members' financial capacity. However, they were concerned to avoid a perfect one-to-one relationship between financial capacity and influence in the club. On the one hand, members taking greater risk ought to have substantial say in the rules and practices of the club—if only to secure their continued financial commitment. On the other hand, the overwhelming financial capacity of a very few countries to take that risk, if reflected fully in the allocation of votes, would undermine the spirit of a club. As Harry Dexter White noted at the time (referring to the International Monetary Fund), "to accord voting power strictly proportionate to the value of the subscription would give the one or two powers control over the Fund. To do that would destroy the truly international character of the Fund, and seriously jeopardize its success."[9] Therefore in the case of the Bank and the IMF the founders introduced such mechanisms as "basic votes" that were distributed equally to all members (in the Bank each member has 250 votes irrespective of shares, plus one additional vote for each share), and double majority voting (of shares and of member countries) to make certain fundamental changes in the Articles of Agreement.

The idea was that the country taking the main risk—at that time the United States—would define the key boundaries within which the club's operations would work. At the same time, to preserve the spirit of a club and to ensure that the club would be effective, other members, including active borrowers (initially the Europeans) would have opportunities to influence, within those boundaries, the club's specific priorities, policies and detailed practices, and on some key issues, the ability to resist changes that might reflect only the narrow interests of a few powerful members.

Over time, however, whatever ability and interest the Bank's initial mostly European borrowers had to affect the Bank's priorities, policies and practices have clearly eroded for today's many more numerous borrowers. In 1947–1948 the Bank made loans to six countries (France, the Netherlands, Denmark, Luxembourg, China and India). Today the IBRD and IDA lend to almost 150 countries. And the world has changed in another respect. Political mechanisms of representation and voice in "democracies" and in international "clubs" of nations are now almost universally acknowledged as ideal in their own right (*Development as Freedom*, to use the title of Amartya Sen's book), and as effective in an instrumental sense—for sustainable growth and poverty reduction because they create accountability and produce checks on abuse of power. The idea of political freedom in a democracy is also now closely associated with the Western economic model of open markets, and thus with the original "mission" of the club. International clubs are not immune from these changes in norms.

The result, reflected in the report and essays in this book, is a growing demand for reform of governance at the Bank, especially to ensure much greater representation— in terms of voting power, Board membership, staffing, and so on—of developing country borrowers who are the members most affected by Bank policies and practices. The spirit of an international club is particularly resonant in the proposals for:

- The current president of the Bank to "push the Bank's member governments to make the Bank's governance more representative and thus more legitimate" and commit now to a more open and transparent process for selection of his successor (Working Group Report).
- Use of double majority voting on many more issues to create an incentive for borrowers who now see no point in debating institutional issues over which they have no influence to build coalitions (Ngaire Woods).

- A governance structure for a trust fund for global public goods at the Bank in which the middle- and low-income borrowers would have at least 50 percent of the votes, with the middle-income countries having more power to set the agenda in return for the financing they would be providing by paying higher interest charges on their loans than otherwise (Working Group Report).
- A rethinking of the "framework" for the IDA window, separate from any reconfiguration of IBRD shares (which would have little impact on decision-making in the IDA), so that both donors and recipients would "feel more ownership" (Masood Ahmed).

With a more representative governance structure and broader engagement of borrowers, the Bank would obviously look more like a club, and looking more like a club would command more legitimacy as a global institution. It would still be a credit club, in which the big depositors have more say. But it would also provide much greater incentives for borrowing members to engage on key issues. To quote Harry Dexter White once again: "Indeed it is very doubtful if many countries would be willing to participate in an international organization with wide powers if one or two countries were able to control its policies." [10]

2. The low-income countries: Is the Bank effective?
Masood Ahmed in his essay makes the point that without reform of its governance, the Bank risks additional erosion not only of its legitimacy but its effectiveness: "I am persuaded that the World Bank cannot continue to deliver the results we all want over the next decade without substantial governance reform." [11] Ngaire Woods also links the Bank's problems of effectiveness to its inadequate governance: "current arrangements have proven to be ineffective from a corporate governance point of view as well as from a political 'legitimacy' point of view."

Ahmed is referring primarily to the Bank's efforts to end poverty, particularly in the poorest, most aid-dependent countries. On that effort, William Easterly goes further, arguing that the Bank is already failing to deliver results— failing because it lacks mechanisms of accountability for results to the poor people whom it is meant to be helping. For Easterly, lack of accountability is rooted in the lack of political voice of the poor—of their countries in the Bank, and in many cases of the poor in their own countries.[12] Steven Radelet is equally critical of the Bank's effectiveness in the poorest countries most dependent on the Bank, saying that the Bank encourages recipient governments to "take on way too many issues and activities, leading to no focus, no sense of priorities, and less progress on really key issues."

The Bank, along with virtually all official creditors and donors, is now committed to the principle of "ownership" by developing countries of their own policies and reforms. Yet as long as the Bank itself is not seen as "owned" and legitimate in developing countries, it is too easy for Bank-financed programs to become controversial and difficult for developing country leaders to implement. The plight of Bank adjustment programs (and of the much benighted "Washington Consensus" reforms in general) is a compelling example; Easterly (2002) among others document their failure in many low- and middle-income countries. Bank programs become controversial not only because they have losers as well as winners (which cannot be avoided), but because they are seen as imposed from outside.

Returning to the spirit of Bretton Woods might help. In a club (but not in an aid agency), the recipients of financing have the power that comes with membership, and their agreement is more obviously required on the broad policies and practices that govern the financing process.

3. China, India and the middle-income countries: Is the Bank still relevant?

It could be argued that since the IDA window for the low-income countries is financed by contributions from the rich countries, IDA is the "aid agency" of the Bank. But that is not the case with the IBRD window, the source of financing for China, India, and most of the world's "middle-income" countries (in World Bank parlance, countries with income above $825 per capita). The club-like nature of the Bank rests largely on its IBRD functions.

Adam Lerrick argues persuasively that the Bank should shift its resources from loans for middle-income countries to grants for the poorer countries, on the grounds of the "irrelevance of lending" in a world of sophisticated private markets. He and others point to the decline in borrowing and the acceleration of loan repayments by many middle-income countries in recent years. On at least that score, for at least one country right now, he has a point: "China is awash in money."[13] David de Ferranti answers, equally persuasively, noting the volatility of markets, the poor access of some of the smaller and poorer "middle-income" countries and the broad-based analytical knowledge the Bank brings to issues of global importance, such as financial crisis prevention and environmental protection. The Working Group Report adds the argument of the legitimate interest of the rich country non-borrowers in promoting equitable growth in countries where two-thirds of the world's poor live, including in support of their own prosperity and security (pp. 21–22 in this text).[14]

De Ferranti and the Working Group Report make various proposals for retaining the allegiance of middle-income borrowers (and thus retaining access to the net income their borrowing generates), emphasizing the need both for new products to catalyze private flows to countries, and for reduced costs of the "hassle" associated with borrowing from the Bank, be it due to: excessive (or not) fiduciary obligations including to limit corruption, excessive (or not) safeguards against environmental and other costs, or the political and financial costs of excessive (or not) delays between requesting and receiving a loan. Similarly, Jessica Einhorn (2006) suggests that the Bank's members agree to lock in now a 25-year sunset clause for loan disbursements, as an incentive for the Bank management and bureaucracy to adapt itself to the creative challenge of developing a new set of non-loan services for middle-income countries more quickly.

If we conceive of the Bank as a club, managed by its members for their own benefit, then the substantive merits of these arguments and proposals for change, one way or another, yield to the question of whether particular members wish or not to avail themselves of the benefits their membership provides—under existing conditions—and/or use their influence to change the conditions. If China wants to borrow at the cost already agreed to by all the members, for whatever reason (including because China trusts more the technical input of the Bank if it is bundled with a financial commitment), then so be it. If a country (Korea in 1998) that had eschewed borrowing for many years asks the Bank for a loan during an emergency, then so be it. If non-borrowers wish to limit the subsidy implied in loans to relatively rich or more liquid (in terms of reserves) middle-income members, then they have the option of proposing a policy of smaller subsidies (higher interest charges on loans) for the relatively rich borrowers.[15]

Put another way, let the members of the club decide. In effect that is the current situation—though it reflects as much the inertia of failed cooperation as a positive decision. An interesting issue arises because some members, and particularly the borrowers, have limited influence in changing the conditions (pricing, delays, conditionality, and safeguards) under which they now participate as members. In that sense, the governance question—whether the Bank can return to its roots as a global club—is key to whether it continues to be relevant in its current form for a large group of its members. In the absence of voice, some members may in effect choose the option of exit.[16]

4. Global public goods and independent evaluation: Is the World Bank a "knowledge bank?" Would a "knowledge bank" be more relevant?

The Working Group Report suggests the Bank is uniquely positioned for greater strategic involvement in the production and financing of global public goods. It is so positioned both because of its potential to finance production of such goods (including by others), and because of its combination of a global "macro" perspective on the costs and benefits of such goods with specific technical expertise in relevant sectors, such as agriculture, health and environment. Michael Kremer provides four compelling examples where the Bank ought to be active: health and agricultural technologies for the poor; an African road network (co-financed with the African Development Bank); financial support for countries that take in and integrate refugees; and the development of global knowledge on the impact of various public policies in developing countries.

Certainly, greater involvement of the Bank in global public goods, with agreement on priorities by the members, makes sense. (At the moment, the Bank does have programs in global goods, but they are financed and managed in an *ad hoc* way, often relying on special contributions from one or two rich country members.) A program of support for global public goods would enliven the "club" spirit at the Bank. That would be particularly so were it supported, as recommended in the Working Group Report, through a large, new trust fund financed by direct contributions from members (presumably mostly non-borrowers), and by pre-agreed annual transfers from net income due to the Bank's loans—implying indirect financing by Bank borrowers. A separate financing and governance arrangement would in effect constitute a new club within the existing club.

The question, however, is whether the Bank as an institution does currently gather and convey useful "knowledge" on development practice. On the one hand, supporters of the Bank increasingly invoke its comparative advantage in generating and disseminating worldwide knowledge and expertise on development policy and practice. The Working Group Report, for example, refers to the Bank as "development's brain trust" and as a global public good (pp. 17–18).[17] On the other hand, others are deeply critical. Devesh Kapur asks whether the Bank's spending on the production and dissemination of knowledge is cost-effective relative to direct spending on other global public goods: "If the Bank's overall budget was cut by a third and the resulting savings (more than one half billion dollars annually) were put into research in those diseases, crops and energy technologies that are *sui generis* to poor countries, would the global welfare of the poor improve or decline?" He links the virtual absence of Bank reliance on researchers based in developing countries to Bank researchers' greater interest in "propositional" knowledge—the search for universal laws of development—and "prescriptive" knowledge, rather than in "a deeply textured knowledge of the circumstances" of a country that could provide guidance on how to build institutions and who might do so.

Levine and Savedoff worry, in a similar vein, that "the Bank rarely creates new knowledge about what works." They describe a track record that is "wanting" on the very sort of program that Kremer calls on the Bank to support: impact evaluation of programs in developing countries.

To address the effectiveness of the Bank as a knowledge bank, Levine and Savedoff call on the Bank to encourage and support much more impact evaluation, including of the programs and projects it finances, and to join in a collective response to ensure "supply of knowledge, a global public good in the truest sense." Kapur wants more outsourcing of research and knowledge creation to scholars based in developing countries, and more emphasis on the production of country-specific knowledge. Kremer calls for more direct financing of research in agriculture and health likely to have global benefits, presumably including research done primarily outside the Bank. Pierre Jacquet calls on all donors and creditors, including the Bank, to agree on benchmarking of their programs against results of evaluations.

But (as Kapur notes) there are now no incentives for the Bank, as a bureaucracy, to outsource research. Indeed, short of specific contributions for specific programs, the Bank as a bureaucracy has no incentive to "do" global public goods beyond its own in-house "knowledge" activities. And as Levine and Savedoff note, there are disincentives for Bank staff to promote impact evaluation of Bank-financed programs. Under current conditions, it is not clear that the Bank can be an effective "knowledge" bank, even regarding learning about its own effectiveness. (Nor is it clear that under current bureaucratic incentives, Easterly's and Radelet's worries that the Bank is not accountable for results and not able to set priorities in low-income countries, or the complaints of others that the Bank creates too much hassle for middle-income borrowers, will be addressed.)

But perhaps proposals to exploit and to fix the Bank as a "knowledge" institution could be realized in a more club-like environment. The development literature is now replete with invocations of the simple reality that developing countries are ultimately responsible for their own fates. Accountability for results of development efforts must rely ultimately on the political mechanisms by which governments are accountable to their citizens and by which international institutions are accountable to their members. A club might more obviously create accountability of its staff to all its members.

To argue that the Bank explicitly recognize its potential comparative advantage as a "club" is not to suggest that it become less businesslike. Indeed, an alternative metaphor for a more effective and relevant Bank, that of a competitive firm subject to market discipline, leads to much the same conclusions about the need for reform. Mark Stoleson, of a global private investment firm, makes this point with unusual freshness and clarity in the final essay of the volume "The World Bank: Buy, Sell or Hold."

A concluding note

In any event, it is an over-simplification to call the Bank a club. Yet the implication of the various arguments in this volume is that in the 21st century, the Bank will not thrive as an aid agency and that a continuation of business as usual (a mix of functions and practices and habits responding to multiple and varied demands, summarized as "mission creep") would deprive the global economy of its continuing need for an institution dedicated to shared prosperity.

The Bank is unlikely to achieve "relevance" in this more global system, or "effectiveness" in helping countries transform their economies, without the elusive "legitimacy" it seems to have lost. The one step to furthering all three— effectiveness, relevance and legitimacy—would be to ask how as a club it might better serve all its members—rich and poor.

Notes

1. Allan H. Meltzer, chairman, *Report of the International Financial Institutions Advisory Commission* (Washington, D.C., 2000). Also available at http://www.house.gov/jec/imf/meltzer.pdf.

2. On the burden on developing country officials of dealing with the resulting "cacophony" of donor voices, views and demands, see Arnab Acharya, Ana Fuzzo de Lima and Mick Moore, "The Proliferators: Transactions Costs and the Value of Aid," IDS Working Paper (Sussex, U.K.: Institute of Development Studies, 2003).

3. The relevance of the non-borrowers' guarantees to the bank's ability and cost of current borrowing rate is sometimes questioned, since the bank's financial policies since the early 1970s have included substantial provisioning and reserves, and since it has been so rare that borrowers have delayed repayment let alone

defaulted. Since more than 80 percent of the IBRD's current reserves come from transfers from net income and only a small minority from paid-in capital, there is a sense in which the borrowers can now be said to be contributing to the bank's low borrowing cost and financial solidity. Of course from the beginning the guarantees were, like the nuclear option, only useful when not used.

4. Jessica Einhorn, "Reforming the World Bank," *Foreign Affairs* 84, no. 1 (2006): 18. The full quotation is "Its core mission is no longer to partner with middle-income countries in their pursuit of balanced and externally oriented growth; it is to alleviate poverty in poor countries and in the poorest pockets of middle-income countries." I have omitted words to clarify that the key distinction of interest is between partnership for externally oriented growth and poverty alleviation—not only or necessarily between middle-income and low-income countries.

5. Nancy Birdsall and Devesh Kapur, co-chairs, *The Hardest Job in the World. Five Crucial Tasks for the New President of the World Bank*, in this volume, p. 15.

6. See, for example, the World Bank Operations Evaluation Department (OED), *2004 Annual Review of Development Effectiveness* (Washington, D.C.: World Bank, 2004). The OED has now been renamed the Independent Evaluation Group (IEG).

7. The debate about poverty or growth is often decried as silly; for a good statement see Dani Rodrik, "Growth Versus Poverty Reduction: A Hollow Debate," *Finance & Development* 37, no. 4 (2000). Birdsall refers to "conditionality confusion" and suggests that conditionality and ownership are complements, and not in any way substitutes. See Nancy Birdsall, "The World Bank of the Future: Victim, Villain, Global Credit Union?" Carnegie Policy Brief No. 1 (Washington, D.C.: Carnegie Endowment for International Peace, 2000).

8. See the Working Group Report in this volume for more detail and for citations to these critiques.

9. Joseph Gold, *Voting and Decisions in the International Monetary Fund: An Essay on the Law and Practice of the Fund* (Washington, D.C.: International Monetary Fund, 1972) p. 19. White's statement is referred to in this context by Ngaire Woods, *The Globalizers: The IMF, the World Bank and their Borrowers* (Ithaca, New York: Cornell University Press, 2006).

10. Gold 1972, p. 19.

11. Ahmed invokes Kemal Dervis, who provides an extensive discussion and examples of how lack of legitimacy is eroding effectiveness of the Bretton Woods institutions. See Kemal Dervis with Ceren Ozer, *A Better Globalization: Legitimacy, Governance, and Reform* (Washington, D.C.: Center for Global Development, 2005).

12. See also William Easterly, "What Did Structural Adjustment Adjust? The Association of Policies and Growth with Repeated IMF and World Bank Adjustment Loans," CGD Working Paper #11 (Washington, D.C.: Center for Global Development, 2002).

13. See also Jeremy Bulow and Kenneth Rogoff, "Grants versus Loans for Development Banks," Paper for AEA session on New Perspectives on Reputation and Debt, January 7, 2005.

14. In addition to the Working Group Report, in this volume, for a set of arguments see Nancy Birdsall, "The World Bank of the Future: Victim, Villain, Global Credit Union?" Carnegie Policy Brief No. 1 (Washington, D.C.: Carnegie Endowment for International Peace, 2000); and José Angel Gurria and Paul Volcker, *The Role of the Multilateral Development Banks in Emerging Market Economies: Findings of the Commission on the Role of the MDBs in Emerging Markets* (Washington, D.C.: Carnegie Endowment for International Peace, 2001).

15. A key rationale for the recommendation of the Gurria-Volcker commission of differential loan pricing was to encourage graduation of richer borrowers with access to private markets.

16. The risk that China and other Asian nations will set up a regional monetary fund is the key impetus currently for the United States and Europe to agree to some change in IMF quotas. A similar situation might arise at the Bank, though in less dramatic form and creating less immediate pressure on non-borrowers.

17. See, among others, Linn, who refers to the Bank's function as a "transmission belt" to carry low-income countries through middle-income status into the ranks of higher-income countries; Johannes. F. Linn, "The Role of World Bank Lending in Middle Income Countries"

(comments presented at the OED Conference on the Effectiveness of Policies and Reforms, Washington, D.C., October 4, 2004), p. 3; and de Ferranti, in this volume, who refers to the Bank's "broad-based analytical expertise on development policy issues" and its ability to "combine an appreciation of the broad macro perspective with detailed examination of policy issues at the sectoral and micro levels."

Votes and Voice: Reforming Governance at the World Bank

by Masood Ahmed

My objective here is to spark discussion about the future governance of the World Bank group. This is a large topic and one on which much has been written. I am going to focus mainly on the role and composition of the Board and its relationship with management, but I recognize that there are also many other aspects of the corporate governance agenda for the IFIs.

Why Governance Matters

A legitimate initial question is whether improving the governance of the World Bank is a priority issue for delivering better development results for the world's poor. I start from the premise that the World Bank is the single most important international actor in the development business: ensuring its effectiveness over the coming decade is a high priority for development policymakers in rich and poor countries alike. And I am persuaded that the World Bank cannot continue to deliver the results we all want over the next decade without substantial governance reform.

There are two broad sets of arguments that drive the improved governance thesis. The first posits that voice, legitimacy and effectiveness are mutually reinforcing attributes for an international development organization, not competing objectives.

Kemal Dervis, Administrator of UNDP, has argued powerfully for the enduring merit of the U.N. in terms of global legitimacy—including in a presentation to CGD. He extended this line of argument to the Bretton Woods institutions. In order for them to be a fully credible source of advice, and for their advice to be backed by conditions which would carry sufficient political acceptance to be workable, he saw the need for a much greater sense of

Masood Ahmed is a national of Pakistan and holds an M.Sc. in Economics from the London School of Economics. At the time of this symposium, he was a Director General at the United Kingdom's Department for International Development. He has also held several senior positions at the World Bank, and at the IMF where he currently serves as Director of the External Relations Department.

87

their acceptance in the broader international community, and particularly in developing countries. This acceptance, he argues and I agree, is intimately bound up with their legitimacy, in terms of how their governance is structured and how that is perceived. So the argument is that it is not good enough simply to have the right policy advice; that advice is more likely to be accepted if it comes from an institution that is seen as representative of the interests of the borrowing countries.

These arguments apply to the World Bank's work in both middle-income countries, mainly through the IBRD, and in low-income countries, mainly through IDA. A further argument for improving developing country voice in IDA stems from the 'development coordinator' role that it plays for the broader donor community.

I now work for DFID. And right across the countries where we operate, I am struck by the fact that there are multiple donor interventions in the same area, overlapping with each other, creating extraordinary demands on scarce national administrators' time and trying to get them to focus on each donor's strategic plan, each donor's set of conditionalities, each donor's set of operating specifications. Moreover, these countries frequently don't have the capacity to handle all these burdens simultaneously. Middle-income countries usually do, but many low-income countries, particularly in Africa, lack the capacity to be able to provide a framework within which each donor could operate in a highly complementary way with the others and the national authorities.

Fortunately we are beginning to recognize the cost imposed by this lack of harmonization and alignment. Our pledge to do better is enshrined in the 2005 Paris Declaration on aid alignment, harmonization and results. However, this will be a long-haul endeavour, and for many aid-dependant countries I see IDA as providing essential backstopping to help governments to provide a framework within which all donors can operate. Of course, IDA will not be expected to do this alone—we need to understand better how the U.N. system, the Bank, the European Commission and a few well-positioned bilaterals can be complementary—but it will be asked to take on at least an important, highly visible and exposed supporting role in very many country situations.

To play that coordinating role effectively, IDA needs to enjoy external legitimacy, first and foremost with the countries where it plays this role. It also needs to earn and maintain legitimacy with other key development partners and, significantly, opinion-shapers in donor countries including in civil society.

A second important lens through which to consider governance of the World Bank is from the perspective of recent experience with corporate governance in the for-profit and non-profit sectors. In the corporate world, governance has evolved a long way in the last 20–30 years, as witnessed, for example, by the report of the Cadbury Committee in the U.K. on this subject a few years ago. While there is no cookbook recipe for governance of a major corporation with many diffused shareholders and millions of stakeholders, and no two situations are entirely alike, there are some basic principles which command widespread respect.

A key one is the importance of a relatively clean delineation between the functions of management versus non-executive directors (confusingly "executive" directors in the Bank parlance). As Sir Adrian Cadbury pointed out when he met informally with the Bank's Board two years ago, this basic requirement is not yet met in this institution. More generally, it is not clear whether directors are primarily operating in the narrow national shareholder interest or for the wider corporate interest, and if the latter, whether the process by which they are appointed, retained and rotated favors or hinders this perspective. Another obvious, and much analyzed, issue is the role and selection of the Bank's President, who combines, U.S.-corporate style, the roles of Chairman and CEO, an increasing anomaly on the other side of the Atlantic. Therefore, both the changed international development context and lessons from corporate governance argue for change at the level of the Bank.

Building on Progress

The excellent recent report on the Bank by CGD identifies some immediate improvements that are desirable and feasible. Let me simply outline them before suggesting two more fundamental ideas for change in the medium term which need more exploration.

The first is to pursue disclosure more vigorously. The Bank has come a long way in terms of disclosure, but there's still more that we can do to disclose country strategies, and especially country level policy and institutional assessment ratings. There are some valid arguments for caution where the information may be politically or market-sensitive, but the presumption must be that these ratings can and should stand up to challenge, and that sharing them increases the likelihood of positive emulation. Over time, there is a case for progressively externalizing the assessment function, using standards developed by the Bank and other financiers against which countries can then be benchmarked.

The second is the issue of decentralization. There should be continued decentralization of decisions as far as possible to country level, both in terms of continued "deconcentration" of staff responsibilities within the institution, but also by making more space for effective decision-making by countries themselves. The latter kind of decentralization requires everyone— including shareholders—to accept a greater relativism of policy options, to recognize that there are usually several feasible adjustment paths from one situation to another, and that weighing the pros and cons of each is a sovereign matter. If the Bank, and for that matter the Fund, come to be seen as more respectful of country voice and ownership in this more fundamental sense, this will improve governance and legitimacy in a major way even without formal changes in the Washington-based superstructure. This is significantly about changing the day-to-day behavior of Bank staff, and so would require a hard look at the Bank's personnel management and incentive framework.

The third area is trust funds, official-speak for widespread *ad hoc* financing of the institution outside of its core resources from capital and retained earnings or, in the case of IDA, periodic core replenishments by donor countries. I find it extraordinary that in a recent year the World Bank received a larger sum of grants from its shareholders in trust funds than it got for IDA. Some of this money is for big multi-donor initiatives channeled through the Bank (such as HIPC) or cofinancing for specific Bank operations, but a substantial amount is for supplements to the Bank's own budget for policy or operational work. It is remarkable that as shareholders we construct an elaborate mechanism for setting priorities and discipline in the Bank, and then as donors we bypass this mechanism by setting up specific separate financial incentives to try to get the Bank to do what we want. Inevitably this is sometimes different from what the Bank's Board, on which we put our director, has just instructed it to do.

This is not unique to the World Bank by any means—in the case of several U.N. agencies the accumulation of such non-core or "project" funding has been larger overall than core funding for years. And it is true that these projects, on the whole, meet specific operational needs and achieve results at their own level. But this constant, sprawling, decentralized process of contracting for parallel funding has a corrosive long term hollowing-out effect on corporate governance. The pendulum has swung too far in this direction and is overdue for a correction.

My fourth area for action is independent evaluation. This is important in its own right as a key tool for improving our understanding of what works in development, as we discussed in another session in this conference. It also has a huge payoff in terms of improving the legitimacy of the policy prescriptions that come out of the institution that is rigorously and publicly evaluated, in this case the World Bank. It therefore enhances the process of governance reform we have been discussing. I should note that a focus on impact evaluation will also help to raise the priority of improving the current woefully poor quality baseline for development indicators in many developing countries.

These are the types of immediate improvements we should move forward on. But there are two more radical questions which I'd like to explore.

The first question is whether it's time to revisit this model of a 200-person plus resident Board. It results in an extraordinary degree of involvement of the shareholders in the day-to-day management of the institution, wherein the lines between management and shareholders begins to blur.

Few corporations would consider having a permanent resident Board of directors, let alone one like the Bank's which costs tens of millions of dollars a year to run, and requires heavy dedicated management infrastructure to service its requests for information. Even in the esoteric world of public development finance institutions, especially those created since the 1990s, this is a rarity. More often in similar institutions, shareholders interact mainly through brief periodic meetings of senior officials from capitals. They can bring a more direct and authoritative connection with domestic priorities, while complementary checks and balances—such as robust oversight committees on policy or top management appointments—operate outside of the Board itself. I surmise that if the Bank were re-created today, we would not invent anything like the governance infrastructure that we have inherited. It's not obvious to me that moving over immediately to a smaller, nonresident, non-executive board is the only or best answer. There may be other solutions that have equal merit. But the issue does need to be joined. First, for cost reasons: taxpayers have a right to get value for money. But also to get clear lines of corporate governance responsibility.

The second question is: how do we introduce more voices from developing countries in the different decision-making processes in and around the Board? Over the past five years, there has been considerable work on this, with proposals both covering the recalibration of relative shares and voting rights and the suggestion to add one or two African chairs to the Board to increase the voice of the poorest countries. However, we are still short of a consensus. Are we trying too hard for a one-size-fits-all, comprehensive governance solution?

I'm beginning to come to the view that we have two different problems of inadequate developing country voice which need tailored solutions. One is that the emerging markets don't have adequate representation from their perspective in IBRD, which is a kind of market-based cooperative, of which they are an integral part. That's a different issue from the fact that the poorest countries, particularly in Africa, who are the primary beneficiaries and recipients of IDA financing, don't have enough voice in the IDA decision-making process.

The IDA problem is compounded by the role of IDA Deputies, who increasingly set the framework within which IDA operates, subject to later validation by the Board with limited further debate. Although there are now half a dozen borrower representatives as nonvoting observers in the IDA Deputies' meetings, they do not have anywhere near the kind of intervention and capacity to shape the policies of IDA. Donors have a right to insist on value for money for their taxpayer investments in IDA, but they should also get the best possible inputs from recipient countries in determining what is and is not effective, and this is not yet happening. Moreover, when IDA management responds to Deputies' (i.e., donor) requests for policy papers, IDA recipients feel their ability to shape the product is limited and *ad hoc*. Some have also called for more of a challenge function, by asking for ideas also from Southern development thinkers for the Board and Deputies to consider.

If the formal Board voting structure were really the essence of the problem, there are plenty of technical solutions at hand. As Nancy Birdsall has pointed out, the Inter-American Development Bank has a formula of full parity in its voting between developed and developing countries. Others—for example, IFAD with its three tiers of capital representing recipient countries, OECD, and non-OECD donors—have found solutions that fit their political needs. IDA itself has already provided for a potential voting split which, while not quite 50-50, could go up to 48 (low and middle-income) to 52 (high-income). This would involve poor countries taking up additional, heavily discounted shares long reserved for them. The reason they do not is revealing, and is arguably not primarily about cost as this would be quite modest and could presumably be subsidized further if needed. Rather it is because small changes in the IDA voting shares alone would not affect important decisions, such as constituency composition which is driven by IBRD shares, or the relationship with IDA Deputies.

So the question that we should be asking is whether this diverse set of issues—including the under-representation of the emerging markets in IBRD, and how IDA recipients influence the shaping of IDA policies—can all be done by trying to reconfigure shareholdings and/or adding a couple of seats to the board of IBRD. I am increasingly skeptical that a silver bullet exists.

Perhaps we need to step back and think more fundamentally about whether we need a new framework for the business of IDA, which brings in the donors to IDA and the recipients of IDA, in a better-structured conversation. They could shape rules and operating criteria in which they would all feel more ownership.

This should be accompanied by a separate discussion about the nature of emerging markets participation in the market-based cooperative of IBRD. They need to come together in a way that would represent ownership from them of the role that IBRD plays in their economy, and that they play in the world economy. This goes back to the early history of IBRD as a cooperative tool for the rebuilding of war-torn Europe, with its quite different dynamic to that of an "aid agency."

I freely admit I have not gone here beyond posing the questions, and am offering no ready-made answers. I also do not have a firm view yet on whether there is likely to be enough political traction in the search for answers. Moreover I fully appreciate how by differentiating between parts of the Bank we could be raising thorny issues about the relationship between these components, with the potential loss of synergies embedded in the current set-up. But I do think that this question of differentiating voice in the IDA and IBRD contexts, along with the question on the future of the non-resident Board, are fundamental and we need to grapple with them.

I look forward to others joining this discussion in due course, and thank CGD for giving the opportunity to contribute these preliminary thoughts.

The Battle for the Bank

by Ngaire Woods

The World Bank will not be able to avoid reform in the immediate period. The powerful requestioning of its sister institution in Washington DC cannot help but spillover onto the Bank. Yet any "governance" reform of the Bank needs undergirding with a clear sense of its purpose and role. At least four kinds of Bank have been skirted around. I suggest that we need a narrower test to guide which of these Banks the World Bank should become.

Reform is in the air

The winds around the Bretton Woods twins bode for change. It is the IMF which is currently in the frontline —not due to rabid criticism so much as a fatal lack of interest. A few months ago I found myself a lone voice among experts briefing the UK Treasury Select Committee about globalization and the UK economy, arguing that the IMF has an important role to play. The IMF has become irrelevant opined the other experts. A few weeks later speaking to the European Parliament, my case for reforming the IMF fell on ears more receptive to the case made by an Argentinian congressman—that the IMF had destroyed Argentina's prosperity. Inside the IMF there is a scratching of heads. Is the public too ignorant or too indifferent about the IMF? "We don't know and we don't care" seems to be the public's response.

Officials most closely involved with the IMF are pushing to change what the organization does and how it is governed. Most recently proposals have been made by the United States, the United Kingdom, and South Africa. US Treasury Official Tim Adams has argued for

Ngaire Woods, Oxford University and Center for Global Development
Ngaire Woods is director of the Global Economic Governance Programme at University College, Oxford where she teaches and supervises research in graduate international relations. She is an adviser to the United Nations Development Programme's Human Development Report Office, a member of the Helsinki Process on global governance, and most recently served on the three person external review panel asked by the IMF Board to review the IMF's Independent Evaluation Office. She sits on numerous editorial and advisory boards, including the Advisory Group of the Center for Global Development. Her most recent book is *The Globalizers: the IMF, the World Bank, and their Borrowers* (Cornell University Press, March 2006).

weighted votes in the Fund to be altered to recognize the growing economic strength of Asian countries in the global economy, as well as for the IMF to have a more ambitious and robust approach to exchange rate surveillance.[1] On governance, more radically, the UK's Central Bank Governor, Mervyn King, recently argued that we should get rid of the Executive Board of the Fund and instead use a non-resident Board meeting six times per year.[2] Meanwhile South Africa's Central Bank Governor has made the case for fundamental reform to give developing countries more voice in decision-making in the IMF, speaking—for all developing countries—of the "highhandness," "know-it-all approach" and "almost patronising attitude towards developing countries" of the institution.[3]

The World Bank will be affected

The arguments for reforming the IMF will affect the World Bank on all three issues highlighted above. First, the allocation of votes in the IMF has long been under question but is now seriously under fire. The World Bank will be directly affected by this debate since its voting structure mirrors that of the IMF. Second, the governance structure and the role of the IMF's Executive Board is rightly under question and this too will translate across to the Bank which has the same basic permanent, resident Board structure. Third, poorest borrowers have long attacked the modus operandi of the IMF and its ideological dogmatism. In its approach to lending, the World Bank has taken serious steps to move away from one-size-fits-all and to devolve ownership to its borrowing members. But has it done enough?

The quest for change in the IMF will doubtless be gingered by the fact that the institution's largest borrowers have been repaying, leaving the Fund short of prospective income. But so too the Bank's traditional borrowers are enjoying access to alternative sources of finance and turning away from the Bank—for reasons spelt out in the CGD's Report on the Future of the Bank. Both institutions are having to explain afresh their raison d'etre. For the Bank this entails asking—what makes us attractive? What do we exist to do?

What should the Bank do?

In and around the World Bank a lot of effort has been put into examining what the Bank does well and how it might compete with other agencies. Yet the Bank is not a private sector institution, nor a national or regional one. It should not supplant the efforts of those competing in the market. It is a public multilateral agency with a fairly universal membership created by governments to fill a need which neither private markets nor individual governments can. What the Bank should be is what it is uniquely placed to do as a universal, multilateral development organization.

The Bank's original mandate was to go where markets were likely to fail to go—or fail to get to fast enough. In 1944 this meant rebuilding Western Europe after the second world war faster than nonmediated private capital would. This would not only ensure economic growth (and a market for US goods), but it would also alleviate social and political fractures which would otherwise take place. The Bank's original mission also included lending to developing countries whose immediate prospects may not attract capital but whose stability and growth were seen as important to global prosperity and growth. Finally, the Bank was born to manage the excesses of the market. This meant working to ensure an even growth of trade so that the benefits of global commerce would raise the standard of living and conditions of labor across member countries. Put differently, the World Bank was created (alongside the IMF) to manage what we now call globalization, and in particular its "downsides."

The original purposes of the Bank did not overlap or contradict with what other international agencies would be doing in the post-war period. Certainly the Bank was born in a period of great belief about what governments could achieve—after the New Deal and amidst the birth of the welfare state in Britain. But in the intervening years the Bank has become more of a jack-of-all-trades. Paradoxically, the expansion of the Bank's activities has taken place alongside a proliferation of hundreds of other multilateral agencies working on the same issues. For this reason it is worth thinking harder about what the Bank should and should not do—as indeed the CGD Report on *The Hardest Job in the World* does. Let me propose here a slightly more restrictive test than in that report, aiming it at four of the kinds of Bank which were touched on in that report.

The Knowledge Bank is the Bank which focuses on high-quality research and its dissemination. Better collection of data, research and sharing of information by the Bank —we are told—will translate into better quality and more even economic growth around the world. The same rationale is used to justify multilateral surveillance and research undertaken by the IMF. The assumption that this role is necessary for each organization to achieve its main goals is seldom tested. Of course knowledge and furtherance of the social science of economics and development economics is valuable, but it is not only the Bank which is engaged in this. So too are the OECD, universities around the world, regional and national policy institutes, and other development organizations.

Should the World Bank be a "Knowledge Bank"? The test is a two-fold one. First, is there something about the way the Bank collects and disseminates knowledge which is distinct from what other research and monitoring organizations can do—and indeed which the Bank is uniquely placed to do? Second, does the Bank's work as a Knowledge Bank contribute directly to its mandate such as by contributing to more equitable and balanced international trade so as to raise "the standard of living and conditions of labor" across all of its member countries (to quote Article 1 of the Bank's Articles of Agreement)?

The Listening Bank is the World Bank of the Comprehensive Development Framework and decentralization. It is a Bank which listens more and imposes less. It puts borrowing governments "in the driving seat" (in spite of the fact that in none of those countries does the boss ever occupy the driver's seat). In some ways the "listening bank" tries to reconcile "ownership" with the Bank's ever-more intrusive presence in borrowing countries. This could improve a number of things about the Bank's performance and knowledge. It could enhance the Bank's understanding of how actual sectors in specific economies work—more useful for the Bank's poorest members than most of the general theorizing done at headquarters. It could inject some humility into Bank projects and policies—rendering the Bank a genuine "development partner." It could also drag the Bank into all manner of projects including democratization and social reform.

Should the World Bank be a "Listening Bank"? Again the test is twofold. First, is the Bank uniquely placed

to engage in processes and policies implied in the
"listening bank" or is it supplanting what other organizations
(public and private) can and should be doing? Second,
will the Bank's listening activities help it to fulfil its core
mandate? I am in no doubt that to some extent they will.
But the risk is that the trend to a greater presence on the
ground will tempt the Bank into an ever wider agenda,
full of good intentions but applying the wrong skills and
expertise to a mission which goes beyond that for which
it is equipped.

The Dams and Irrigation Projects Bank is the Bank
of those who want the Bank to attract back its large-
scale borrowers which give it a raison d'etre and a
healthy income stream. It is also a vision which pushes
back against the Bank's widespread shift into more
easily-disbursed social and sectoral reform lending.
But dams, irrigation and large infrastructure projects
take the Bank squarely into a number of battlegrounds.
Procurement for large infrastructure contracts (including
by the world's wealthiest countries and corporations)
is notoriously rife with corruption and kickbacks. It sits
with difficulty alongside the anti-corruption goals of the
new President. Large infrastructure projects often strip
people of their homes and damage local environments,
leading the Bank into head-on conflicts with NGOs and
local communities which it has been (and still is) trying
so hard to cultivate.

Should the Bank be engaged in large-scale infrastructure
lending? Tough as it may be, this was a key part of the
original mandate of the Bank which includes developing
productive capacity in countries when private capital is
absent or too expensive. The uniqueness of the Bank's
role here stems from its capacity to raise finance more
easily and cheaply than any individual country. But do
its activities in this area contribute to fulfilling the Bank's
mandate? Recall that the Bank's mandate is not simply
to promote economic growth but to promote trade,
investment, and productivity which is balanced and
contributes to better standards of living and conditions
of labor within and across its members. The Bank has
a duty—distinct from the private sector—to ensure that
all people's living standards and working conditions are
bettered. At the very least it should work in ways which

ensure that basic human rights are not impinged. This is difficult but has to be part of what the Bank does.

The Big Expensive Bank. Finally, it is worth mentioning the Big Expensive Bank which has little by way of a hard budget constraint (for increases in costs can be passed on to borrowers). It is a Bank which has spent millions on advice and restructuring within its own walls as each new President has attempted to recreate around himself an institution with which he is more familiar. There is no rationale for an undisciplined Bank. The Executive Board and Board of Governors (member countries) have robust powers of oversight which they can exercise. The problem is that they too seldom, and too ineffectively do so.

Governance reform is inevitable

The Boards of the Bank (both the Board of Governors and the Executive Board) need to act properly as supervisers of the institution rather than micromanagers. Their job is to ensure that the Bank fulfils its strategic goals—defined here in terms of what the Bank is uniquely placed to do. Other contributors have commented on governance reform in the Bank, and I have written extensively about it elsewhere. Suffice to say here that current arrangements have proven to be ineffective from a corporate governance point of view as well as from a political "legitimacy" point of view. The senior management is selected by a process seen as neither fair nor meritocratic by the rest of the world and results in a Bank unduly skewed towards its largest vote-holder. Although small and expert, the Board has not been an effective strategic arm or constraint on the management of the Bank. Nor is the Board seen adequately to represent the full membership of the Bank whether seen in terms of economic weight, affectedness by Bank actions, or contributors to the Bank's expenses.

There are some straightforward solutions to these problems.[4] First, on leadership the President and senior management must be seen as equally accountable to all countries who are members of the Bank. All countries pay for the institutions—they should also all have a say. The Bank sits in Washington DC and therefore is prima facie perceived as primarily accountable to the United States. Its President and Senior Management need powerfully to balance that perception. At the very least the double-role of the US as host of the institution and holder of the Presidency needs reducing by dropping the convention that the US appoints the President or by shifting the Bank's headquarters to another capital (which would be required by the Articles if the Europeans sat with one seat on the Board and thereby became the largest quota holders).

The Board needs to be effective in overseeing and monitoring management, and ensuring that the Bank's core activities adapt appropriately to reflect what the Bank is uniquely placed to do and what contributes directly to its mandate. At present the Board neither represents the Bank's membership adequately nor fulfils these core functions. The Board has eight Directors which directly represent individual countries (United States, France, United Kingdom, Japan, Germany, Russia, China, Saudi Arabia), and sixteen Directors who represent the rest. Most Directors live in a grey zone, based in Washington DC, paid by the Bank, and neither instructed by, nor accountable to, most of the membership of the Bank.[5]

For about 174 members of the Bank, there is little incentive to engage in decisions being made by the Board. This is because eight Directors can marshal a majority among themselves with little if any consultation with others. This does not have to be the case. If Directors had to marshal not just 50% of votes (which might be just 8 members), but also 50% of members (92 countries) to make decisions, there would be a clear incentive to consult and bring on board Directors who represent a large number of countries but wield few votes (such as the two Directors who represent over twenty African countries each yet each wield less than 3.5% of voting power). This is not a difficult reform. The Bank's Articles already provide for double-majority voting (Article VIII) for any amendment to the Articles. This could be extended to other decisions. Along with transparency of the Board's process such as publication of the full minutes of any Board meeting so that countries can read exactly what their Director has said in Board meetings, these would be first steps towards a more effective Board.

In brief, reform is in the air around the IMF and World Bank in Washington DC—and so it should be. Powerful members of the Bank should be pushing a new more effective structure of governance, and a strengthening of the <u>unique</u> contribution the World Bank can make to the equitable spread of globalization and economic growth.

Notes

1. Timothy D. Adams (US Department of the Treasury), The US View on IMF Reform, Speech presented at the Conference on IMF Reform, Institute for International Economics (Washington, D.C., 23 September 2005).

2. Mervyn King (Governor of the Bank of England), Reform of the International Monetary Fund, Speech given at the Indian Council for Research on International Economic Relations (New Delhi, 20 February 2006).

3. Tito Mboweni (Governor of the Reserve Bank of South Africa), Speech at University of Pretoria (Pretoria, 28 February 2006).

4. These are elaborated at greater length in chapter 7 of Ngaire Woods, *The Globalizers: the IMF, the World Bank, and their Borrowers* (Ithaca, New York: Cornell University Press, 2006).

5. For a closer analysis of the functioning of the Boards see Ngaire Woods, "Making the IMF and World Bank more accountable," *International Affairs* 77, no. 1, (January 2001): 83–100; and Ngaire Woods and Domenico Lombardi, Uneven patterns of governance: how developing countries are represented in the IMF, *Review of International Political Economy* 13, no. 3 (August 2006): 480–513.

The World Bank and Low-Income Countries: The Escalating Agenda

by William Easterly

I have a very simple message about the World Bank and low-income countries. To be effective, the World Bank needs to have in place a set of tasks, a mission, and an incentive system that will create accountability for results. Accountability for results implies that there will be some reward for getting results and some penalty for not getting results. That's the first message.

The second message is dispiriting. The World Bank in low-income countries is now and has been for a long time suffering from a really bad case of mission creep. Such mission creep has taken it farther and farther away from tasks on which it is even feasible to have accountability. To reverse that trend is really the first step in having a World Bank that is accountable for achieving results in low-income countries.

Let me tell you what I mean by "mission creep" and how this is a long-run tendency. There have been a lot of interventions that have been tried, and these interventions have been unsatisfactory, leading the World Bank to try an ever more ambitious and extensive set of interventions in an attempt to make up for the failure of the previous interventions. To get concrete, in the early days, The World Bank was all about roads, dams and schools. The mentality was, if you build it, they will come—by doing specific projects that would create tangible outputs.

To be fair, there was some success in that period. There were successes at building roads, dams and schools. There were successes at building infrastructure for clean

William Easterly, New York University and the Center for Global Development
William Easterly is Professor of Economics (joint with Africa House) at New York University and a non-resident fellow at the Center for Global Development. He spent 16 years as a research economist at the World Bank. He has worked in many areas of the developing world, most extensively in Africa, Latin America, and Russia. His areas of expertise are the determinants of long-run economic growth and the effectiveness of development assistance efforts. He is the author of *The Elusive Quest for Growth: Economists' Adventures and Misadventures in the Tropics* (MIT, 2001), *The White Man's Burden: Why the West's Efforts to Aid the Rest Have Done So Much Ill and So Little Good* (Penguin, 2006) and numerous articles in leading economics journals and general interest publications.

water, and indicators of access to those services have actually gone up in Africa. In fact, one of the success stories that is not talked about enough in the literature is that there have been some major achievements in Africa and they usually have to do with the specific project tasks that used to be the main mission of the World Bank.

There was also a certain level of dissatisfaction that such specific projects did not bring rapid development to Africa, and so then we move to the next phase. The idea took hold that to be effective, project interventions needed to take place in the presence of good macroeconomic and microeconomic policies, mainly free markets, free trade, low government deficits, macro stability—the Washington consensus. This line of thinking brought us to the age of structural adjustment.

The World Bank, beginning in 1980, started making loans conditional on adopting a large number of policy reforms in an attempt to redress what was perceived as a gap in the previous effort, or as a reason why the previous effort failed: that the interventions were not themselves enough to create development, because if the overall policy environment was so badly distorted, then development would not happen.

Unfortunately, structural adjustment did not work. Growth did not happen. Policy reforms were very erratic and uneven. The consensus in the scholarly literature currently is that, overall, structural adjustment lending failed to attain its objectives.

If you want to go beyond the scholarly literature, then there is a simple stylized issue of real import, which is the main topic on the agenda of the IMF-World Bank meetings this weekend, and that is debt relief.

Debt relief is talked about as sort of this benevolent thing that rich countries are doing for Africa, but what we forget is the flip side of debt relief, that debt relief is really a sign of the failure of structural adjustment.

It is precisely those countries that got a lot of structural adjustment loans that became HIPC (Heavily Indebted Poor Countries), and thus found themselves in need of debt relief. The fact that they could not pay back zero interest loans with a 40-year maturity is itself a completely compelling sign that structural adjustment lending had failed in these countries.

That is true not only of the obvious failures that had negative growth in Africa (which are the majority of those who received structural adjustment loans). It is also true of those that are touted as success stories of structural adjustment—countries the likes of Uganda and Ghana are also getting debt relief. Even the success stories have not been able to pay back structural adjustment loans.

Then we have the next wave of escalation, which maintained that if policies were not the answer, then institutions must be, meaning that the task of international agencies like the World Bank should be to try to promote change and progress in institutions.

There are also various kinds of new vehicles loosely related to promoting institutions, like the new poverty reduction strategy papers, and, in general, all kinds of initiatives to try to promote institutions. I have difficulty understanding exactly how these initiatives are supposed to work, for the simple reason that no one really knows how to change institutions from the outside.

We can think of specific piecemeal things that would change institutions for the better. However, we really do not yet know how to achieve a wholesale transformation of institutions. The evidence that we have is that, if anything, aid leads to a worsening of good governance in recipient countries.[1]

That is essentially where we are now, except in some countries there has even been a further step, indeed an even more ambitious one, which is in the states that are called "failed states." It is in these countries where we have even more escalation, where international organizations would actually take over some of the functions of government and have some kind of new trusteeship type arrangement in failed states. This is exceedingly difficult, no doubt, and yet a further escalation of the current thinking that if we can't change institutions from the outside, let's ourselves become the institutions and take over.

What, then, is going on here? Why do I say that escalation has taken us farther, and taken the World Bank ever farther and farther away from being accountable?

Well, there are two big problems with this escalation. One is measuring results and the other is what the results depend on. Measuring the World Bank's effort and second, what the outcomes depend on. So you can see with each successive step, it becomes more and more difficult to measure the World Bank's effort.

It was easy to measure the World Bank's effort when it was just building a road or building a dam—something highly visible, that could be monitored and accounted for—and it would be very embarrassing if the World Bank gave money for a road and it was not built.

With structural adjustment it became much more difficult to hold the World Bank accountable for the goal of changing policies and the effort that goes into changing policies.

Of course, the natural question is: how do you measure what policy would have been without World Bank intervention? How do you actually measure changes in policies? Policies are a very ill-defined set of lots of different actions.

With institutions, it becomes even more difficult to measure progress, and of course with post-conflict reconstruction, where you're trying to change everything, then the game is up and it becomes hopeless to try to measure the World Bank's contribution.

The second problem for accountability with the mission creep of the World Bank is that with each step of escalation the results depend on more and more factors besides simply what the World Bank does. When the World Bank is building a road, the outcome mainly depends on the actions of the World Bank itself. The World Bank can pretty much determine whether a road gets built or does not get built.

Yet with changes in policies, there are now many actors trying to influence the country to change even more policies, and more so with institutions. Such changes depend not only on outside factors but also domestic political factors, meaning that it becomes increasingly routine to escape accountability because if something goes wrong, everybody can point fingers at everybody else.

The World Bank can say it is the IMF's fault, the IMF can say it's the World Bank's fault, or they both can say it was the recipient government's fault. Alternatively, the recipient government can just say it was the fault of politics that left them powerless.

Blame can also be leveled against outside factors like a hurricane or terms of trade shock, meaning that nobody can be held accountable for the results in these areas. So it becomes overly burdensome to simply hold the World Bank accountable for efforts in these areas.

To make matters worse, with each step it becomes more difficult to prove that the World Bank can even affect these outcomes. With infrastructure projects, for example, it is fairly obvious that the World Bank can build a road, if it wants to. There may be problems with maintenance, but those problems could be solved with particular measurable efforts.

The evidence on changing policies is much weaker. Pretty much the result is, aid does not change policies. The evidence is also such that aid does not change institutions, at least not for the better. It may change them for the worse, and God only knows what we may find ten years from now of the effect on post-conflict countries, of whatever the effort of the World Bank was.

With all of these problems, it seems we have moved ever farther and farther away from accountability. What needs to happen to reverse this trend of escalation and why has escalation happened?

Let's go back to the scholarly literature on development. One thing emerging more and more from the literature is that aid, and outside actors like the World Bank, cannot achieve development and transformation of other societies like poor countries in Africa. This is still a very controversial conclusion but seems to be borne out by a lot of evidence, such as the poor track record of the escalating interventions.

Development and transformation is just something that outside actors cannot achieve. They do not have the tools, the ability, the incentives, and accountability in place to do so effectively. Even if they did have the incentives and accountability, it is not clear that outsiders like the World Bank can achieve wholesale transformation of another society like the complex societies in low-income Africa.

Does that mean that all is lost? No. There are still a lot of good things that aid can do. Aid can do those small piecemeal things like building roads and maintaining them, like getting 12-cent medicines to children who would otherwise die from malaria, like sinking boreholes and getting clean water so that people don't get sick from contaminated water.

Aid can do small-scale things like the current project in the World Bank on the costs of doing business, in which you try to take specific piecemeal steps to lower the red tape of doing business in developing countries. Doing this creates opportunities for what is the real engine of development and transformation in low-income countries, which is the private sector and it's the homegrown efforts of local people themselves, both political leaders and private sector within African countries, within low-income countries themselves.

That is where development and transformation is going to come from, not from the outside actors.

If the World Bank is willing to focus on those more modest tasks, then feedback and accountability is feasible and the World Bank could achieve better results. If the aid community focused on these smaller tasks and held the World Bank accountable for achieving those results the roads that are not being maintained now actually could be maintained. The 12-cent medicines that are not reaching the children dying of malaria could reach the children dying of malaria, if the aid community focused on simple tasks like that and held the World Bank accountable for those tasks.

Otherwise, development will happen mainly because of what Africans do, because of what people in low-income countries do, and not because of what the World Bank does.

Notes

1. See Stephen Knack, "Aid Dependence and the Quality of Governance: A Cross-Country Empirical Analysis," Policy Research Working Paper 2396, (Washington, D.C.: World Bank, 2000).

The Role of the Bank in Low-Income Countries

by Steven Radelet

This note makes four brief points about the role of the World Bank in low-income countries. The first point concerns mission creep, or lack of institutional discipline. The Bank is involved in too many activities in individual countries and does not have a particularly clear focus. This lack of focus and overextension transfers to the recipient country governments who are encouraged by the Bank and other donors to take on way too many issues and activities, leading to a lack of focus, no sense of priorities, and less progress on a small number of really critical issues.

The Bank does this partly because it has, in house, a wide range of expertise and a decentralized structure so that it tends to try to support all kinds of activities. The main concern is not necessarily that the Bank globally has expertise in too many areas and needs to narrow its focus as an entire organization, although that is an issue. The more important problem is that within individual countries it has difficulty focusing on the really key issues, deciding that some problems cannot be solved right away, and determining a small number of very high priorities. It needs to do a much better job of both setting its own priorities within countries and helping recipient countries think through their priorities.

As a result, the Bank and other donors also tend to encourage an attitude of trying to solve all problems at once. It is very easy to go into a low-income country and find 25 or 50 or 60 problems, and to tell the recipient country that X is not working very well, we've got to fix Y, we've got to change Z, and so on. While it is true that these may all be problems, there is no sense of priorities; the problem is that in developing countries, the scarce

Steven Radelet, Center for Global Development
Steven Radelet is a senior fellow at the Center for Global Development, where he works on issues related to foreign aid, developing country debt, economic growth, and trade between rich and poor countries. He is co-author of *Economics of Development* (a leading undergraduate textbook), and author of *Challenging Foreign Aid: A Policymaker's Guide to the Millennium Challenge Account* (Center for Global Development, 2003).

resource is strong government policymakers, meaning that there are only so many things that can be tackled. The real challenge in development policy is not finding problems, but determining which problems should be solved first, given limited resources, to get the biggest bang and set the stage for continued change.

The good news is that to achieve development, we do not have to solve everything at once. If you look at the countries that have been successful over the last 40 years, mostly but not exclusively in Asia, they have not solved everything at once.[1] Take China as an example. No one would argue that China has solved everything at once. Nor have Korea, Indonesia, Malaysia, Botswana, Mauritius or Chile.

These and other successful countries were able to set priorities and get a few critical things right, and really solve some of the most pressing problems, rather than attempt to solve a wide array of problems simultaneously. Unfortunately, the Bank and the donors do not do this very well. Most specifically, the World Bank's Comprehensive Development Framework is a mistaken approach, because it encourages the attitude of "let's try to solve everything at once and fix all of these problems because development is so complicated," rather than "let's set some priorities and try to make real progress on the most important issues first, and follow on with others later."

Second, the Bank and other donors have to do a better job of recognizing that not all developing countries are alike, and it is necessary to differentiate the strategies that are used within developing countries. Here I am not making the point that the substantive development priorities differ across countries, which they obviously do, but rather that the quality of governance, commitment to development, and institutional capacity differ widely across countries, so the approach the Bank takes should recognize these differences, and the Bank should more clearly vary the way it provides its assistance across the spectrum of countries. There has been a lot of talk in the last few years about selectivity, the principle being that we give more aid to countries with better governance and institutions and less to countries that don't perform as well. This is a sensible starting point, but we need to go beyond that and actually *deliver* aid differently to countries that have different capabilities and qualities of governance.[2]

For example, in recent years there has been a lot of talk surrounding the issue of budget support, about country ownership, about longer-term commitments, about all kinds of things, as if these are the right solutions for *all* developing countries. But they are not. The principle of country ownership may not be appropriate under certain circumstances. Zimbabwe, with its current destructive government, is a perfect case in point—no donor should give more ownership of the development program to the government of Zimbabwe, and none really does. But our rhetoric about improving aid effectiveness does not take these differences into account, and implies that changes that make sense in some countries are a good idea for all. Donors, including the World Bank, need to move beyond the general rhetoric and shift toward thinking about how to employ different kinds of approaches and modalities in different countries. In countries that have better governance, better institutions, and have shown some commitment toward progress—countries such as Ghana, Honduras, Mongolia, Mozambique, Senegal, and Tanzania—it makes sense to have more country ownership, to provide longer-term commitments, to send more of the money through the budget as budget support, and otherwise change the ways that we deliver assistance.

In countries with weaker governance, we should stick with more project support, look for a narrower set of activities, and have a mix of donor priorities and country priorities. In countries with the weakest governance, there should be a much narrower set of activities, much less government ownership and involvement in setting priorities, a shorter time frame, shorter time commitments, much tighter oversight in what is done, a different way to measure results and different ways of delivering money, with less of it through the government and more of it through non-governmental organizations.

We have to shift toward creating these more distinctive strategies for different countries. Donors are beginning to move a little bit in this way, in some cases implicitly and in others more explicitly. The United Kingdom's DFID and some other European donors are providing budget support in some countries but not in all (although the criteria they use to make these distinctions are not clear). The United States has set up the Millennium Challenge Account, which very explicitly distinguishes among recipient countries. And there is some welcome movement within the Bank along these lines, but it needs to go further in providing its assistance in different ways across countries. The Bank's increased use of grants opens many new possibilities that it has not yet begun to explore about to whom and how it provides financing under different circumstances.

Establishing more distinct modalities could help create incentives for countries to strengthen governance and institutions. Budget support provides a good example. It makes sense for the Bank to provide budget support in countries that have better public sector finance institutions, stronger fiduciary standards, and better accounting and auditing practices, but not in countries with weaker systems (note that this is not the same as better governance more broadly). There are now many ways of ranking and grading public sector finance institutions, such as the budget office and the ministry of finance more generally. The Bank should use such grading systems, and provide a greater share of its funding as budget support to countries that score better on these standards. For example, as governments reach a certain standard on auditing, accounting, publishing their accounts, procurement, and other areas, they receive some share of their funding as budget support, say 20 percent. As their standards improve, they could receive 50 percent or 75 percent or more. Note the issue is not about how much money they would receive, but *how* they would receive it. The incentive would be built in for the countries to want to improve their systems, because by doing so they could receive more of the money in the way they want it—as budget support.

The third point is on accountability. The Bank currently does not reward results strongly enough, and too often it rewards failure. It needs to be much more results-oriented. To its credit, the Bank has begun to move in this direction in recent years. But it is a huge challenge to try to change incentives within an institution, and to try to reward success rather than failure. Part of the answer is in removing long-standing incentives for Bank staff that are focused on disbursing money, and creating incentives that are connected to the success or failure of the activity. But these changes will not just happen by people saying we ought to do a better job and we ought to focus more on results and by hoping staff respond. Instead, changes must come from the Executive Board and from senior management who must make structural and policy changes that create incentives that are focused on results. Management could make proposals to the Board for re-orienting staff incentives and promotion over time so that they are more linked to results, or to how projects are monitored and evaluated over time to focus on results. Similarly, Board members—both contributors and recipients—could demand more results-based approaches.

The United States has been pushing from the Executive Board to hook its IDA contributions to broad indicators of the Bank achieving results. I am generally supportive of this approach, although I have not agreed with all the details of how it has been carried out. It would be better if these kinds of initiatives primarily came from management rather than the Board. It will also be a challenge to translate these kinds of measures from an institution-wide focus to specific projects and programs.

President Wolfowitz has made the point about the need for the Bank to be more results-oriented, and hopefully he will be able to move the Bank in this direction. One key in focusing more on results, as proposed by my colleague Nancy Birdsall, would be the creation of a truly independent outside evaluation entity that can measure results on specific activities and for the Bank more generally.[3]

The fourth and last point concerns grants. From the Bank's perspective, providing more of its assistance to low-income countries as grants makes a lot of sense, but the way the Bank is allocating grants across countries doe not make much sense.[4]

When the shift to grants began in 2002, the Bank decided to allocate grants based on sector—certain activities, such as health education received more grants, while others such as infrastructure were financed by loans. It quickly became apparent that this formulation would not work, as countries would receive mixes of grants and loans, leading to incentives to move money and creating confusion.

More recently, the allocation rule was changed so that the share of grants a country receives is based on measures of debt sustainability. The rationale seems simple: grants were pushed by the United States and others partly as a solution to sustained debt problems, and giving grants to countries with the largest debt problems certainly helps reduce their future debt burden. But basing grants on debt sets up strong perverse incentives, because the more debt a country accumulates, the more likely it will be to receive grants, whereas the more a country manages its economy well and avoids debt problems, the more it will be told that it must continue to borrow. This rationale does not make a lot of sense, especially as we are about to forgive all the debts for countries that reach the HIPC Completion Point, meaning that those countries will be prime candidates for more loans, rather than grants.

Instead, grants should be based on a country's income. The poorest countries in the world should get grants, and as their incomes grow, they should receive more loans—first subsidized, and later not subsidized. That's the principle the Bank uses to distinguish between IDA and IBRD funds, and that's the way most donor flows work. As incomes grow and countries achieve higher incomes that demonstrably prove a greater ability to service debt, the level of concessionality should decline.

The poorest countries in the world are the ones that face the deepest development problems, so they face the greatest risk that they will not be able to achieve the growth necessary to repay loans, even if they establish good policies. They tend to be vulnerable to the greatest number of shocks and face the largest obstacles to growth. When they do achieve growth, the resources should be reinvested, not repaid to the Bank to be relent elsewhere.

Going forward, the Bank should set up either a third separate window or a window within IDA for grants only for all countries with incomes below $500 per capita. This would ensure that the poorest countries receive the most concessional money and do not face debt problems. As incomes grow in these countries and they begin to show some capacity to actually get returns on investments, they can go to IDA loan-financing. This approach will better match grant financing with the greatest needs, and avoid the perverse incentives of allocating grants based on debt.

Notes

1. See Steven Radelet and Jeffrey Sachs, "Reemerging Asia," *Foreign Affairs* 76, no. 6 (November/December 1997): 44–59.

2. Steven Radelet, "From Pushing Reforms to Pulling Reforms: the Role of Challenge Programs in Foreign Aid Policy," in *The New Public Finance: Responding to Global Challenges*, eds. Inge Kaul and Pedro Conceição, (Oxford: Oxford University Press, 2006). Also available as CGD Working Paper #53 at http://www.cgdev.org/Publications/index.cfm?PubID=196.

3. Nancy Birdsall, "Seven Deadly Sins: Reflections on Donor Failings," CGD Working Paper Number 50, December 2004.

4. See Steven Radelet, "Grants for the World's Poorest: How the World Bank Should Distribute Its Funds," CGD Note, June 2005, http://www.cgdev.org/content/publications/detail/2681.

Has the World Bank Lost Control?

by Adam Lerrick

"We are facing...competition [from the capital markets]. I think it's important that we effectively compete. Increasingly,...if the fight against poverty is successful, more and more countries will be in this middle-income category, and if this institution is going to remain relevant to the world, it obviously needs to be relevant to the middle-income countries."

World Bank President Paul Wolfowitz, September 22, 2005

The World Bank is in big trouble. Major middle-income countries, the cream of the Bank's portfolio, are curbing their borrowing and paying down their balances, setting off alarms at the Bank. Net loan flows have shifted $30 billion over the last seven years, from positive to negative. Instead of drawing a net $14 billion from the Bank in 1999–2002, these nations repaid a total of $15 billion in 2003–2005. The cause is clear: The interest subsidy embedded in Bank loans, a compelling 12 percent per annum on average in 1999, has now shrunk to less than 2 percent as emerging nations have gained increasingly greater access to private capital. The difference is no longer enough to persuade finance ministers to realign their economic priorities with the social agendas of the Bank's rich members.

For years, the Bank has been in the business of lending at highly subsidized rates to non-needy nations. Ninety percent of Bank loans now go to just 27 borrowers, 10 of these accounting for 75 percent, a list that closely parallels private sector choices, and for these nations the Bank contributed a mere 1 percent of the average

Adam Lerrick, Carnegie Mellon University and American Enterprise Institute

Adam Lerrick is the Friends of Allan H. Meltzer Professor of Economics at Carnegie Mellon University and director of the University's Gailliot Center for Public Policy. He is also a Visiting Scholar at the American Enterprise Institute. His published papers include "A Leap of Faith for Sovereign Default: From IMF Judgment Calls to Automatic Incentives", "The World Bank as Foundation: Development without Debt" and "Bank Deposit Receipts: A Transitional Money for Financial Crisis". Lerrick is an expert in monetary economics, international finance, financial markets and the role of international financial institutions in the world economy.

net $200 billion that the capital markets have provided each year over the last decade.

When the International Bank for Reconstruction and Development (IBRD) was founded and its self-image formed, capital markets were small, segmented and cautious. The Bank was to borrow in the markets, backed by the AAA guarantee of its rich industrialized membership, and lend on to developing countries that could not access resources to fund growth. International financial intermediaries to channel funds and assume risk were in short supply. The plan was for developing economies to be nourished only until they had gained the financial credentials to attract private capital on their own. This was called "graduating." But the Bank won't let go.

The Bank was enjoined from displacing the private sector. Now it wants to compete. With its monopoly power lost, the Bank is scrambling to maintain market share by lowering prices. In the end, it is the demands that are at the very center of its mission that will be sacrificed to maintain competitiveness.

Middle-income borrowers are clearly good for the Bank. The Bank wants to keep its best, lowest risk customers. Their loans are more likely to be paid and their projects more likely to succeed. Without these prime clients to raise the value of its portfolio, both its credit and its credibility would be challenged. And the Bank has been willing to pay for the privilege of "staying involved." Over the past twelve years, IBRD loan revenues have fallen short of administrative costs by a cumulative $3 billion. Over time, more and more countries will move into the middle-income group that already commands two-thirds of World Bank Group money and effort.

But is the World Bank good for middle-income borrowers? The Bank's litany of reasons for lending is refuted by the facts of the market place. Its premise of a shortage of private funding is no longer valid. Its business model that relies on subsidized financing is outdated. Its advice now has a negative value to its best clients. In a world of finite aid resources, its money and effort are better dedicated to the poorest nations whose access to private capital is in the distant future.

The global economy has out-distanced the need for World Bank lending to emerging nations and along the way has done more to alleviate poverty than all the interventions of officialdom. But if the Bank insists, and its rich members concur, that a First World vision should be imposed on a developing world and that the poor must be elevated whether they live in countries that cannot afford to pay or in countries that do not want to pay, it needs a new financial structure to match modern realities.

Six World Bank Pretexts for Lending

The Bank wants to remain "relevant" to the middle-income countries but its defense of lending as a means to "stayed involved" is rooted in the past and now refuted by the facts.

I. The Bank lends to countries without ready access to the capital markets

It is widely believed that the World Bank devotes the greater part of its effort to countries denied market financing. In truth, the Bank centers its portfolio on the most credit-worthy candidates, a broad overlap with the private sector that is specifically enjoined in its mandate.

A review of the Bank's lending over the last five years reveals that 99 percent went to countries with international bond ratings from an investment-grade A down to a high-yield/higher risk B. Approximately 25 percent of resources flowed to nations with an investment grade rating and an additional 74 percent to countries with high-yield ratings at the time of the loan. More disquieting, the share of IBRD loans to countries without international ratings has fallen from 40 percent in 1993 to 1 percent in 2001–2005. (See graph I.)

The Bank has contrasted the private sector's 70 percent concentration of flows to 10 countries with its own lending spectrum that channels resources to the entire developing world. However, a review of the major recipients of the IBRD's resources over the last five years reveals that 10 countries accounted for 76 percent of flows, while the remaining 69 borrowing members were left to divide only 24 percent.

These are the very countries that attract the bulk of private sector resources: Turkey (14 percent), Brazil (13 percent), India (10 percent), Mexico (9 percent), China (8 percent), Argentina (8 percent), Colombia (5 percent), Indonesia (3 percent), Romania (3 percent) and Russia (3 percent). (See chart I.) There are another 17 emerging nations with reliable access to the capital markets.[1] Added together, just 27 economies monopolize 90 percent of Bank lending.[2]

In total, the 10 major borrowers received $2 billion in net resources from the Bank over the past five years, or an insignificant 0.4 percent of the $580 billion originating in private sector medium- and long-term external debt, portfolio equity and direct investment.[3] (See chart I.)

II. The Bank lends where the developing world's poor live

As emerging nations have gained increasingly greater access to financial markets, the Bank has conjured up an alternate argument. It is the relative share in the developing world, whether by population, by economic size or by poverty that justifies the concentration of its lending in so few major emerging countries.

The numbers deny this claim. Six of the Bank's 10 leading clients annexed 52 percent of Bank loans over the past five years, yet only accounted for 10 percent of the total population and 24 percent of the GDP of IBRD-eligible borrowers. Their average per capita income of more than $8,000 on a purchasing power parity basis placed them in the top quarter of emerging nations. (See table I.)

III. The Bank lends for projects without interest to the private sector

A host government guarantee is required on all Bank loans. This displaces private sector lending dollar-for-dollar for any country with capital market access and renders the destination of proceeds irrelevant. When private lenders can look to the host government for repayment, as the Bank does, the capital markets are indifferent to end-uses. Whether the goal is financing vaccinations of Indians in the Amazon or nuclear weapons, prospectuses of sovereign bond issues simply state "general government purposes" as the use of proceeds.

IV. Bank lending is the sole source of funds for long-term development

The benefits of many projects accrue over long-term horizons and were once difficult to finance, even for countries with ready access to the markets. Now, the capital markets supply 20-year, 30-year and even 40-year financing, far beyond the Bank offer of amortizing-loans with final maturities of 15–20 years. During the past five years, 23 emerging World Bank borrowers have issued bonds in the market with maturities stretching into the future 25 years and more, well above the limits of Bank terms.

V. Bank loans are a counter-cyclical balance to volatile market flows

The specter of a sudden exodus by the private markets in times of financial stress in contrast to the loyal and steady flow of Bank funding is a timeworn argument. But counter-cyclical stabilization requires more resources than the Bank can muster. If private flows were to collapse by 50 percent, Bank loans would still represent less than 1/50th of the total capital moving into middle-income economies.

The global marketplace is remarkably resilient. Within three months of the 1997 Asian crisis, Korea obtained $4 billion in the capital markets with medium-term maturities. When Brazil faltered in 1998, the next three months counted 20 issues totaling $12 billion for Latin American sovereign borrowers with maturities of 5–20 years. There was even a $2 billion issue for Brazil itself.

A constant stream of lending in anticipation of the off chance of a temporary fall in private sector flows cannot be justified. When and if a crisis threatens, official funds can be mobilized, but this is outside the mandate of a development institution.

VI. Bank lending to emerging countries generates profits to subsidize poor nations

Regardless of credit risk, the Bank charges the same interest rate to all borrowers, equal to the Bank's own cost of funding in the capital markets, plus a spread of 0.50 percent per annum.[4] This spread, when added to commitment and up-front fees, is claimed to cover the administrative costs of running the Bank and make a profit that is passed on to the poorest nations. Far from generating a surplus for the poor, lending is draining resources. When all is accounted for, the Bank loses money on its loans. For the past 12 years, annual deficits of $100–500 million have resulted in a cumulative loss from lending of $3.2 billion. (See graph II.)

In truth, the Bank earns its net income by using its $40 billion of zero-cost capital.[5] This pool of cash generates between $1.5 billion and $2 billion per annum, depending on the level of interest rates. And this net income is the same whether it is lent to Bank borrowers or simply placed in a portfolio of 10-year U.S. Treasury notes.

The record reveals that the Bank's operating income is a function of the level of interest rates. It closely tracks the return on the Bank's zero-cost capital invested at the 10-year U.S. Treasury rate, adjusted for other income and expense. (See graph II.) If the operating income were derived from the spread on Bank loans, the return would be constant, whatever the fluctuations in U.S. Treasury rates.

Bundling Advice and Loans: An Outdated Business Model

Doing business with the Bank is not just about money. Lending has always been a two-part package. There is a loan at highly subsidized rates, historically 7–10 percent per annum below the market. Clearly a gift. And then there is the "technical assistance" which the Bank insists is highly valued and the very reason clients borrow from the Bank. In short, another gift. Yet the Bank contends that borrowers will not follow the advice unless it is partnered with subsidized loans.[6] At first hearing, all this defies logic and common sense. If the Bank's advice is truly "assistance," why do borrowers insist on being paid to comply?

Translated, this Bankspeak is really about imposing a First World social vision upon an emerging world intent on growth. If the environment must be safeguarded, if workers must be protected, if women must play an equal role, if indigenous peoples must be empowered and if the overriding focus must be on the poor, the trade-off has a cost.

Bundling really means that emerging nations are being paid to execute projects low on national priorities, and that they are being paid to implement projects in a manner that imposes large costs, not just in money but in time and effort, that arms-length market funds do not demand. For decades, finance ministers of developing countries have sat at the table and listened—after all, they were being paid millions of dollars per hour in subsidies to attend the lecture.

But in the past decade, three independent trends have converged to destroy the attractiveness of Bank loans: international capital markets expanded and became willing to take on the risks inherent in developing economies; emerging nations became stronger as sound policies elevated their credit status; and nongovernmental organizations (NGOs) were invited by the Bank to step inside the development aid process as anointed spokespersons for civil society. There are now some 20,000 highly vocal NGOs with a multiplicity of demands that have led the Bank to slight the infrastructure needs high on borrower plans for growth in favor of "social programs" without clear economic yield, and to impose elaborate standards that raise the cost of compliance beyond practicality.

Bank "Advice" Has a Negative Value

Do borrowers come to the Bank for the advice or for the subsidy? Now the facts are in and the debate is ended.

Since 1999, the subsidy in World Bank loans to major emerging market governments has fallen from an average 12 percent per annum to less than 2 percent per annum, as measured by the JP Morgan Emerging Market Bond Index.[7] At the same time, the net borrowing by these nations from the Bank has collapsed from a positive $14 billion in 1999–2002 to a negative $15 billion in 2003–2005. (See graph III.) First, borrowing slowed; then countries moved on to repay loans. The interest rate differential is no longer enough to persuade finance ministers to realign their economic priorities with the social agendas of the Bank's rich members.

When it all adds up, the Bank's "technical assistance" has a negative value to its traditional client states. A new generation of government officials, with PhDs from MIT and Chicago, has done the arithmetic. Borrowing patterns reveal that they rated the cost of Bank "advice" at 3–4 percent per annum. Over time, that amounts to 25–35 percent of loan expense. When the interest subsidy fell below the cost of World Bank compliance, the real subsidy vanished and so did the borrowers. (See graph III.)

The conclusion: For years, World Bank loans have been funding projects that countries didn't think were worth financing out of their own resources or worth the cost of borrowing at a market interest rate. Borrowers are willing to pay the markets 3–4 percent more as the price of independent choice.

The Bank Is No Match for the Markets

The Bank was created to fill a void in the international financial system. Resources and a willingness to assume risk were needed to fuel growth in the developing world. The private sector has now preempted the Bank's role of financial intermediary to emerging nations and is far better at it than the Bank can ever hope to be. Yet the Bank is clinging to its past.

Its traditional tools can no longer deliver the subsidy that keeps it in the game. There is little wiggle room in the 0.50 percent annual charge, 0.25 percent commitment fee and 1 percent up-front fee the Bank adds to its cost of raising money to cover its own expenses. When all costs are counted, the Bank is already losing money on its lending. Cutting down on the burdens of the bureaucratic "hassle factor" will have a minimal impact on the "price" of its loans.

To counter the competitive threat of the private sector, the Bank is ready to abandon the protections that have served it well for decades and to search for innovative financial instruments in the marketplace. But the effective cost of Bank resources to its clients can never be lower than its own cost of funds.

How to lower lending rates? How to assume more risk? How to invent new instruments? These are all the wrong questions. Abandoning the sovereign guarantee, lending to sub-national entities, substituting guarantees for loans, securitizing pools of loans and adding what Wall Street calls the "nuclear waste" to the Bank's portfolio. These are all the wrong answers. Even the most convoluted mechanisms to embed subsidies in new instruments will only lead to hidden but ever-increasing costs for the Bank. And the only outcome will be a growing exposure to risk without compensation to cover losses.

The Bank is rational to consider risk lightly for it is well placed to hide failures in ways that might put a private sector institution out of business and its management behind bars. But the Bank has no regulators. Its skills of concealment were honed in the poorest economies where, for two decades, a system of "defensive lending" miraculously matched the dates and amounts of repayment schedules to "new" loans, creating a perpetual roll-over of defaulted debt. In the end, it was the Bank's rich members that assumed the losses of "debt relief" and restored the Bank's balance sheet.

When the Bank steps out of its protected bailiwick, it is skilled private investors who will profit from the Bank's learning experience. Failures to make allowance for risk in a futile effort to defend market share will be quietly covered up. Bad loans will be hidden and rolled over. Effective resources will be diminished. An invoice for the losses will again be delivered to G7 taxpayers.

The Irrelevance of Lending
The Bank is no longer in a world short of capital. World Bank lending is clouding the landscape and wasting resources. All that the Bank really contributes in a world of sophisticated financial markets is the subsidy that fills the gap between the real cost of projects and what recipients are willing to pay.

As the ratings of middle-income countries climb and their cost of market funds falls, the Bank is being forced to seek the help of other donors to recreate the subsidy once provided by its loans. A pioneering project: The Bank is building schools in China's impoverished Western provinces but the bill for interest charges is being mailed to the United Kingdom, attention Chancellor of the Exchequer Gordon Brown.

China is awash in money. There are $700 billion in foreign reserves stored at its central bank and foreign direct investment adds $60 billion each year to the economy's resources. Because the government can borrow in the markets at a lower cost than from the Bank, and because the Bank is more intent on aiding China's poor than China, the U.K. Treasury agreed to pick up the interest tab on the China loans. In 20 years, when China has paid back three loans totaling $300 million, its cost will have been 55¢ on the dollar. All that China really received and wanted was $12 million in annual subsidies, not $300 million in loans.

If poor children are benefiting, where's the harm? There's no harm if global aid resources are infinite. But the Bank's effort to retain influence with middle-income countries siphons off scarce funds from the poorest. There is also potential for harm if Bank loans free up prospering nations to pursue other ambitions, perhaps nuclear weapons or locking up access to natural resources abroad. (Iran has been the Bank's 10th largest borrower and China the 3rd largest over the last three years.)

If the Bank insists that the poor must be elevated whether they live in countries that cannot afford to pay or in countries that do not want to pay, if it wishes to promulgate costly programs that are of marginal interest to borrowers in the name of a freely interpreted version of global public goods, more and more donor funds will be required to restore the subsidy in Bank loans.

An unsustainable business model must be replaced with a new financial structure that matches modern realities. Lending is a blunt and inefficient instrument. The price of persuasion should be at lowest cost. Subsidies can be individually tailored according to the market borrowing cost of governments and the priority the government places on each project.

There is already $40 billion of zero-cost capital on the Bank's balance sheet as a starting point to endow a permanent foundation that would be invested in the capital markets to generate a stream of subsidies. These would underwrite interest payments on country borrowing in the markets. Over time, rich countries may be asked to contribute more funds.

Otherwise, as more emerging nations move up the credit ladder, donors will be compelled to divert an ever-increasing share of their own aid funds to enhance the appeal of Bank loans. The experiment begun in China will be the prototype as Mexico, Brazil, Chile and others line up for the same deal.

Mechanics should not be confused with the mission. The Bank must accept that it is in the development business, not the banking business. Long ago, they may have been one and the same, but now there are better ways to deliver resources to what the Bank perceives as its real clients, the global poor, and to foster global public goods. If the Bank continues to fight the tape, it will become irrelevant to the purpose for which it was designed.

Graph I

World Bank Loans: 99% to Countries with International Bond Ratings*

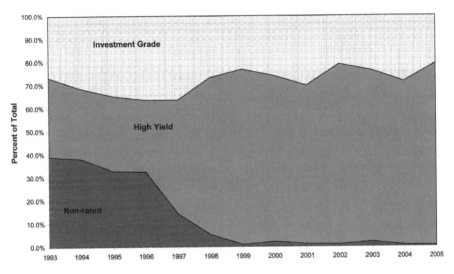

Sources: World Bank, Moody's Investors Service, Standard & Poor's   *IBRD loans excluding Iran.

Chart I

Insignificant to its Major Clients:
World Bank versus Private Sector: Net Flows 2001-2005

Ten Leading World Bank Borrowers

Turkey	14.3%
Brazil	13.0%
India	10.2%
Mexico	8.8%
China	8.2%
Argentina	7.5%
Colombia	5.4%
Indonesia	3.3%
Romania	2.9%
Russia	2.8%
Total	76.4%

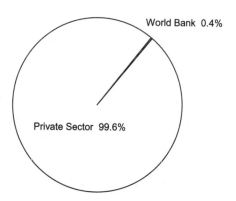

World Bank 0.4%

Private Sector 99.6%

Sources: World Bank, Global Development Finance 2005

Table I

Six Leading World Bank Borrowers:
Bank Loans versus Population, GDP, and Poverty

	% of IBRD Loans 2001-2005	% of IBRD-Eligible 2003 Population	% of IBRD-Eligible 2003 GDP	2003 Per Capita Income (PPP)
Turkey	14.3%	1.6%	3.0%	$6,710
Brazil	13.0	4.1	7.2	7,510
Mexico	8.8	2.3	9.6	8,980
Argentina	7.5	0.9	2.1	11,410
Colombia	5.4	1.0	1.2	6,410
Romania	2.9	0.5	0.7	7,140
Total/Average	**51.9%**	**10.4%**	**23.8%**	**$8,027**

Sources: World Bank, World Development Indicators 2005

Graph II

Source of World Bank Income: Zero-Cost Capital, Not Loans

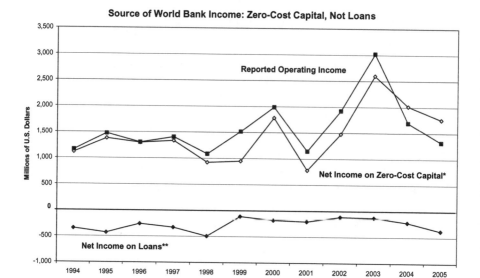

*Estimated based upon the 10-year US Treasury interest rate and adjusted for changes in provisions for loan losses, contributions to special programs, net loan income, arbitrage income and other income to ensure comparability to reported operating income.

**Interest spread income plus commitment fees plus up-front fees on IBRD loans minus IBRD administrative expense.

Sources: World Bank, Federal Reserve Historical Data

Graph III

World Bank and Major Emerging Countries:
Falling Subsidies; Falling Loans

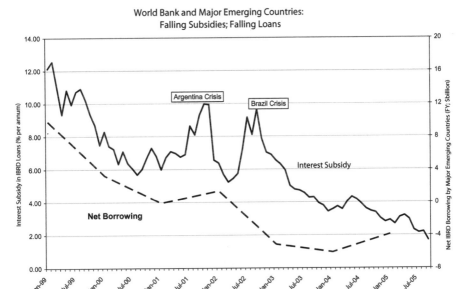

Sources: World Bank, JPMorgan

Notes

1. Bulgaria, Chile, Costa Rica, Ecuador, Egypt, El Salvador, Korea, Malaysia, Morocco, Peru, Philippines, Poland, Slovak Republic, Thailand, Tunisia, Uruguay and Venezuela.

2. Within the middle-income group, there are 52 mostly small economies that may rely on official financing in times of stress. Though significant in number, these nations received only 9 percent of Bank loans over the past five years and account for only 8 percent of developing world population.

3. These figures underestimate the quantity of private sector inflows because the substantial foreign investment in domestic bonds is not included in the data.

4. The interest spread charged on Bank loans was 0.25 percent in 1994–1998, 0.45–0.50 percent in 1999–2000 and 2002–2005, and 0.35–0.50 percent in 2001. In addition, the Bank charges a commitment fee of 0.25 percent and, from 1999, instituted an up-front fee of 1 percent.

5. As of June 30, 2005, the Bank's $39 billion zero-cost capital was comprised of $11.5 billion in paid-in capital and $27.2 billion of retained earnings.

6. Another justification for the bundling is that loans are concrete proof of the Bank's confidence in its own counsel. But the sovereign guarantee on Bank loans divorces project results from the risk of loss. Whether the advice is good or defective, whether the project succeeds or fails, the borrower must repay the Bank.

7. A composite of 19 leading emerging market sovereign borrowers.

The World Bank and the Middle-Income Countries

by David de Ferranti[1]

The World Bank's role in middle income developing countries needs to change. Not to end lending to them, or adopt the other proposals from extremists on the right or left. But rather to *modernize* both what the Bank does and how it does it, so as to respond more effectively to the changed circumstances, needs, and preferences of this group of countries.[2]

Recommendations on how the Bank should modernize are set out below. First, though, the case for it to stay engaged is discussed, since a handful of voices are still trying to argue otherwise.

The World Bank should remain engaged in the middle-income countries

Arguments for axing World Bank lending to middle-ranking developing countries enjoyed short-lived notoriety a few years ago, with the publication of a report by Prof. Alan Meltzer.[3] Since then, however, that fringe view has been endorsed only by a handful of American conservative academics (primarily those who worked on the report in the first place).

Few know this better than Paul Wolfowitz. Nominated in 2005 as the new President of the Bank by a strongly conservative US administration, of which he had been a key member, Wolfowitz's appointment was initially acclaimed by the critics on the right. ("An inspired choice," wrote Alan Meltzer in The Wall Street Journal on March 18, 2005.) But Wolfowitz didn't fall for their odd theories. In his first Annual Meetings speech in September 2005 he stated unequivocally that "To help the middle income countries grow and prosper, we need to continue to tailor

David de Ferranti, Brookings Institution
David de Ferranti was Regional Vice President for Latin America and the Caribbean at the World Bank until his retirement in 2005. Currently he has positions at the Brookings Institution and the United Nations Foundation, and is the Chair of the Board of the Center on Budget and Policy Priorities. Earlier, he held senior positions in the US government and directed research at Rand. His research and writing have examined both developing country and US domestic issues, and he is an adjunct professor at Georgetown University.

our knowledge and financing to their specific needs."[4] Subsequently, on the eve of a visit to Brazil, he was quoted as saying, "I really want to underscore the World Bank's commitment to Brazil and all the other middle income countries in Latin America..."[5]

Nor is Wolfowitz alone. The Bank's 184 shareholder governments—liberal, conservative, and everything in-between—have had numerous opportunities to review and re-decide the Bank's engagement in the middle income countries. Instead of embracing the terminate-lending schemes, they have repeatedly come down firmly, and as a rule unanimously, on the side of continuing the Bank's important development work—analytical, operational and financial—in this critical group of countries.[6]

Watch out for the spin....

The tiny band of diehards have not helped their case by "spinning" the facts through the use of carefully selected statistics. Here are a few examples.

They claim that IBRD loan demand has collapsed. The truth is different. Figure I below gives the facts: IBRD lending commitments each year over the past 15 years.

Lending shows significant fluctuation. It shot up during 1998 and 1999, when the Bank participated in several crisis assistance packages. Levels then fell back, and for a while were appreciably below those of the early to mid

Figure I

IBRD Commitments
($US Million)

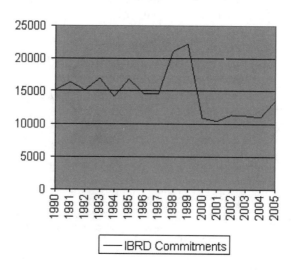

1990s, in considerable part due to a premature cut-back in Bank lending for infrastructure, based on overly optimistic assumptions about the private sector's readiness to pick up this financing responsibility (the infrastructure retrenchment is one the Bank has just recently begun to reverse). The level in the latest completed year (fiscal year 2005) was some 6–7 percent down on that immediately before the 1998–99 crisis. Looking forward, lending in the first half of fiscal 2006 significantly surpassed lending in the same period of fiscal 2005.[7]

How do the spinners transform this rather mundane picture into an Emergency Room? Step one: start the comparison from an atypical base—in this case, kicking off from 1999's record lending. Step two (and more importantly): compare apples and oranges, by mixing up lending with the pre-payment of older IBRD debt. Like many US homeowners, some IBRD borrowers took advantage of recent record low interest rates to refinance their older, higher-interest debt, assuming the opportunity would not last for ever. This is no more an indicator of demand for future IBRD lending than homeowners refinancing their mortgages signals the collapse of the home loan market. In short, if Mark Twain had seen this claim of "collapse", might have been reminded of his remark on hearing that the New York Journal had published his obituary, "An exaggeration."

Another example is the assertion that it is "disquieting" that IBRD lending to countries without international ratings has fallen from 40 percent in 1993 to 1 percent in 2001–05. What this misleading statement obscures is that the number of countries without a credit rating has itself shrunk enormously over the period in question, as more and more countries have sought out ratings. So, a country without a rating is today almost an oddball. Among borrowers from IBRD during the past five years, only 7 unrated countries remained (Algeria, Belarus, Uzbekistan, and four small Caribbean island nations)— they incidentally accounted for less than 1 percent of the IBRD poor. A further dozen non-rated countries were non-borrowers from IBRD, due either to the absence of a supportable program or to having been in "non-accrual status"—i.e., not up-to-date in servicing their debts to the Bank—such as Zimbabwe, for example. The critics' disquiet thus looks more than a trifle overdone.

Still another example is the claim that IBRD lending
largely by-passes the countries where the poor live. In
fact, the top 10 borrowers from IBRD over the past five
years, mostly among the largest countries, together
accounted for about 84 percent of all the poor people
(under $2 a day) living in the MICs as a whole (a further 5
percent of the MIC poverty was accounted for by Pakistan,
an important World Bank Group "blend" borrower, but
one that largely borrows from IDA). (See Table I.) Even if
one cherry-picks the list, as the critics sometimes do, to
remove the four big borrowers with the largest numbers of
poor (China, India, Russia, and Indonesia), the remaining
six countries still accounted for about 22 percent of the
IBRD poor living outside the four giants and got just over
50 percent of the lending. Beyond this, there can be good
reasons for IBRD support even in countries that are not
among those with the most poor people. A country in the
midst of a crucial reform program—such as some of the
former Soviet bloc countries—might want and need help,
and the world (and their poorer country neighbors) might
be better off if they got it. Overall, though, IBRD lending
comes much closer than the spinners acknowledge to
matching concentrations of dire poverty.

Juggling the data also hides something much more
important. When the options and their pros and cons
are even-handedly examined in balanced, reasoned
debate, there are compelling, broad-based reasons
why it makes sense for the Bank to stay engaged in the
middle income countries. Extensive work has been done
examining the reasons.[8] A later section here outlines that
terrain, reinforcing the conclusion that the Bank should
stay engaged. Prior to that, the real aim of this chapter
takes center stage: how should the Bank improve?

How the Bank should modernize its work in the middle-income countries

Modernize Financial Products

Borrowers report that, while the Bank's traditional loans
may have once been appropriate, the institution now
needs to realize that new and different instruments may
be more responsive to their needs. These arguments
need to be listened to.

The Bank has in fact significantly modernized its product
offerings. However, many of these new products do not
appear, at least until very recently, to have been promoted

very actively. Whether one is talking about guarantees, lending in local currency, or insurance products—or the possibility of lending to sub-national levels of government without necessarily requiring sovereign guarantees— more could be done.

The Bank should also look seriously at recent advances in financial markets. This includes "structured finance" approaches where its participation could leverage in far more capital—tapping much more of the huge private sector potential to help development—than is possible through old-style, go-it-alone projects. Proven products take a diversified pool of investments, unpack the risks, and repack them into different tranches matching the risk/reward appetites and capabilities of different classes of investors. The Bank should review whether it should take positions in these areas. In addition, there may be other, perhaps better options out there for vehicles whereby the Bank could leverage greater flows from the private sector.

Cutting Down the Hassle

Many observers—and especially borrowers—feel that the steps and requirements that must be complied with to obtain a Bank loan are still crushingly burdensome, despite recent efforts to lighten the load. The Bank Group needs to take a new look at this "hassle factor."

To some degree, these demands represent a prudent concern to ensure due diligence. "Safeguard" policies, in particular—in areas like a project's environmental impact or effects on local residents such as indigenous people—largely reflect the lessons of experience, and the need to take reasonable precautions. Yet there is also the danger that, under the influence of single-issue pressure groups, agencies like the Bank take refuge in demanding ever-more studies.

The key point here is to make sure that the substance of key risks is addressed—and suitable risk mitigation strategies adopted. But, especially when dealing with more sophisticated borrowers, the Bank should be more willing to work with countries' own national systems of safeguards, where these achieve substantively comparable protection to the Bank's own procedures, and should focus on "upstream" remedies of root causes rather than downstream fixes to projects that are already well advanced. Resistance to this approach by some shareholder representatives suggests a failure to think the issue through properly.

Learning from Differences across Countries

The Bank should review with some care—and aim to learn from—the variations in its client relationships as between one middle income country and another (and one region and another). Some countries and regions have shown continued strong demand for World Bank products, in others interest appears to have weakened. Are the differences inherent to the countries themselves? May some of the differences reflect alternative strategies the Bank has adopted across different regions and countries?

Experience of working in Latin America, for example, prompts the question of how far the Bank's successful efforts to appoint a substantial number of managers and senior staff from within that region may have helped keep the Bank relevant to borrowers' needs. The ability to identify with borrowers and their culture—and speak their language, literally and figuratively—may be one key to staying relevant.

Performance-Based Lending

The argument for providing more support on a "performance-based" basis is compelling. The basic concept is simple. Rather than financial flows being triggered by a country's "inputs" (such as its own spending on health), the performance model ties funding to "outputs" or performance indicators, such as the number of children immunized.

The main issues are practical, not "ideological": how to set meaningful performance indicators, establish reliable systems for monitoring them, make sure no essential components get missed out (such as focusing so heavily on "new" coverage that one neglects to measure upkeep of existing systems). They are not easy challenges, but they should be tackled.

Loan Terms

Some commentators have proposed considering further differentiation of loan terms for different countries. One line of argument calls for stronger, richer countries to pay more, since they are better able to pay. Another makes the converse argument—that the less creditworthy should pay more because they are a worse risk. Elements of both arguments are in fact embedded in current pricing policies. The difference between IDA terms and IBRD terms applies the first argument—the poorer pay less. The harder-than-normal terms adopted for "special" lending—under emergency conditions—requires riskier lending to carry a higher price.

Both Bank officials and the critics agree that current IBRD lending terms are hardly softer (if at all) than those the best-rated borrowers can obtain from the markets. In addition, IBRD loan spreads over the Bank's cost of borrowing are already reckoned to more-than-cover the direct costs of the Bank's "banking" business and to make a hefty contribution to the cost of such "public goods" functions as research and analysis. One might ask how much more of these overhead costs should reasonably be included directly in loan charges.

The trump card in this debate is that the Bank generally revises its basic policies only on the basis of a broad consensus among the shareholders. And consensus on further change in this area will prove hard to come by. Nevertheless, the shareholders have a responsibility to try their best to overcome differences between them, and thus should ask for a systematic look at the issue.

Expanding Intellectual Partnerships
Finally, while the Bank has definitely come some way in combating the "not invented here" syndrome, there is still a way to go. Experience suggests that the Bank still under-uses intellectual capacities outside the institution. There has been an explosion in the numbers of highly-trained professionals in many borrowing countries, and in the capacity of domestic think-tanks, consulting firms, research institutions, and university departments. There is still room for more analytical work to be done in partnership with local organizations. This can benefit both sides—building local capacity further, and improving the quality of the analysis by incorporating different perspectives. A Bank that partners more with others—in earnest and not just in rhetoric, and draws on (and scales up) ideas developed by others—might also be a Bank that does not need as many staff and as big a budget for them as it would otherwise. Certainly, the composition of the staff would need to change, all the more so if the other recommendations here were adopted, especially the one on financial products.

Other actions too have been widely proposed that would help, including some relating to the composition, role, and budget of the Bank's Board of Executive Directors, and others on improving evaluation of Bank operations. There is not space here to go into all of them,[9] but one overarching point is fundamental.

Modernizing the Bank thoroughly will require contributions by everyone—its President, managers, staff, and external groups, but *especially by its member country governments themselves, both through their positions on the Board and at the higher levels where major global policy choices are decided.* For too long, the vital role of the member countries' leading officials and representatives in determining what the Bank can be and do—and the impossibility of bringing about major change in the Bank without their active leadership—have been greatly under-recognized, especially by those not extensively familiar with the inner workings of the Bank. And for too long too, member countries' leaders have failed to find ways to grapple effectively with some of the biggest and toughest questions about the Bank and its future, including the question of its role in the middle income countries. Piecemeal efforts on selected issues—for example, on the low-income countries and on debt reduction—and through periodic discussions in the G8 and other fora, have achieved notable gains, but also created troublesome inconsistencies. A more thorough grappling with core issues, however hard politically, and however long it may take to be fruitful, is of urgent priority.

More on why the Bank should stay engaged

Returning now, as promised, to the case for a continuing Bank role in the middle income countries, there are several parts to the story, including the answers to two basic questions:

- Should the larger world community—the Bank's shareholders—care about developments in the middle income countries and try to influence them?
- Assuming they do, should they work through official development agencies like the World Bank, rather than leaving the job to market forces and/or making ad hoc institutional arrangements?

To answer the first question positively—as governments around the world have in fact done resoundingly—involves recognizing that we live in an increasingly interconnected world, where developments on the other side of the globe can affect our economic well-being, our health, our security and the global environment our grandchildren will inherit. Old dreams of isolationism look threadbare in a world of globalized production, finance and trade, international terror threats, pandemics like HIV/AIDS and bird flu, and global environmental challenges like loss of biodiversity and climate change.

Indeed, what happens in the middle income countries matters a lot in the global picture:

- The MICs account for around two thirds of the world's total population. Their economies, meanwhile, provide important and growing sources of export demand for the wider world's producers and of potential investment opportunities for other countries' investors.
- The MICs include roughly three quarters of all the people living in poverty (under $2 a day) around the world.
- The MICs are now big enough to create systemic risk in global financial markets. A high proportion of recent global financial crises have originated in MICs like Mexico, Russia, East Asia, Turkey and Brazil.
- On strategic issues, MICs repeatedly emerge as key players (the aftermath of the break-up of the Soviet empire, the turmoil in the former Yugoslavia, tensions in the Middle East and South Asia, etc., etc.).
- MICs account for an estimated 47 percent of global CO_2 emissions.
- MICs account for over half the world's areas protected for their environmental significance.

So, why then work through the Bank? A modernized, well-functioning Bank, as imperfect as it will always be, can be shaped into the best instrument that the world's countries are likely to have in the foreseeable future for helping achieve at least some of their global objectives. Among its relatively unique combination of attributes for this role are:

- broad-based analytical expertise on development policy issues at the global, regional and national levels;

- the ability to combine an appreciation of the broad macro perspective with detailed examination of policy issues at the sectoral and micro levels, and a proven capacity to take on new challenges;
- extensive operational experience in implementing reform and investment programs in different geographical and sectoral contexts; and
- sufficient financial capacity to be able to match its intellectual contribution with resource commitments that reinforce its partnership with members throughout the implementation phase.

At the heart of the critics' case, though, is the relationship between the World Bank and private capital markets. Repeatedly, they come back to this comparison: lending by the Bank, they say, necessarily crowds out lending by the markets, lending by the Bank is pitifully tiny compared to the scale of the markets, the Bank cannot compare with the efficiency of the markets, the Bank should not lend to countries with access to the markets....

None of this is new. Those who know the Bank expect criticism from both ends of the political spectrum. Critics on the far left accuse the Bank of being a tool for the spread of international capitalism. Those on the right complain that it is not. Of the two, the leftists seem to have the better factual grasp of what the Bank actually does.

Missing the point on public-private complementarity....

Missing from the conservative critiques is any sense of the importance of complementarity between public agencies and private markets. To the critics, any public lending to a country with market access must of necessity supplant private lending dollar for dollar—they see a "zero-sum game". Yet most economists today recognize that efficient private markets do not appear magically, but require supporting public infrastructure, institutional as well as physical. And much of what the World Bank actually does directly helps to improve the climate for private investment:

- The Bank has encouraged and supported countries in implementing trade reforms to open up to greater international competition, and in removing restrictive regulations on inward foreign direct investment.

- In utilities and infrastructure, the Bank has very actively promoted expanding private provision.
- The Bank helps clients strengthen the essential legal and judicial infrastructure for private markets, including the regulatory frameworks that underpin competitive private financial markets It also helps countries confront corruption, which—among its other evils—distorts the "level playing field" needed by efficient markets.
- The Bank's work on national regulatory frameworks—including its annual published comparisons of "Doing Business" in some 155 countries—provide powerful advocacy tools in favor of freeing business from harmful and superfluous regulations.
- The Bank works alongside other agencies, like the IMF, to help countries emerge rapidly from macro-financial crises when they have temporarily lost the confidence of the private markets. Complementing the IMF's focus on rectifying macroeconomic imbalances, the Bank's emphasis is on promoting crucial structural reforms and protecting vulnerable social groups.
- The Bank's work in helping countries improve the education and health of their populations, and upgrade basic infrastructure, provides crucial support for future market-driven development.

Even the most committed advocates of market-driven development may find it hard to object to most of these efforts—which may incidentally explain why the critics devote so little of their prolific output to discussing what the Bank actually does.

Deconstructing the Bank?
A fall-back for the critics is to argue that, even if what the Bank does might not be 100 percent objectionable, the institution itself is superfluous. Everything the Bank does, they say, could be picked up by the private sector. Private markets could lend where the Bank lends (or at least in the more creditworthy countries), and consulting firms could provide any technical advice needed.

At the theoretical level, one can argue for breaking up any complex organization. Why not replace our cumbersome universities by independent tutors, as in the middle ages? Private certification bodies could compete to provide qualifications. College football teams could be sold to the NFL....

As with universities, the case against breaking up the World Bank involves recognizing that "the whole is greater than the sum of the parts". The Bank's global reach, operational involvement and financial strength enable it to serve an unparalleled "global public goods" function as a respected world center of practical development experience, data and information.

Still, why "bundle" technical inputs with finance? Why not just provide technical advice and let countries go to the markets for resources? Experience points to three factors.

First, for many countries, access to the markets is more problematic and variable than the critics admit. They paint market flows as dwarfing official lending, but most private flows go to private investments—car factories, hotels, Cola bottling plants, etc. In aggregate, average private lending for public (or publicly guaranteed) purposes is roughly comparable in scale to the lending of official agencies, including the Bank. But private lending is far more subject to "sudden stops" in crisis times. And for many borrowers, especially those without investment grade ratings, the effective costs of private borrowing can be steep.

Secondly, even if, in a perfect world, sound advice would sell itself based on quality alone, in the real world, the willingness to back substance with hard resources can often be the price of getting through the door to present one's ideas in the first place.

Thirdly, the knowledge that the Bank is willing to commit its resources to a program offers re-assurance that it will not walk away from the borrower. We all know jokes about consultants who turn in their report and then respond "I don't do implementation." The Bank cannot offer that excuse.

This does not imply that the Bank should never offer advice without funding. Indeed it now provides fee-based advisory services to a number of its clients. But a distinction should be made. Analytical work that is essential for maintaining the Bank's "public good" role of reporting on key development issues should continue as part of the essential package of client services. Advice in areas of very specific country interest, by contrast, lends itself to being placed on an optional, fee-based basis.

Who should be able to borrow?

A key element in the public debate is very different views on who should be eligible to borrow from IBRD. The approach taken by the shareholders is summarized in the Bank's 2005 Annual Report:

"In fiscal 2005 countries with a per capita income of less than $5,295 that were not IDA-only borrowers were eligible to borrow from IBRD. Countries with higher per capita incomes were able to borrow from IBRD under special circumstances, or as part of a graduation strategy."[10]

The Bank's shareholders thus base eligibility primarily on a country's overall state of development (as proxied by per capita income). They apply the approach with some flexibility, allowing for a transition process and for special circumstances, as when Korea temporarily returned to IBRD borrowing status in 1997 (three years after "graduating"), when it lost the confidence of the markets during the wider East Asian crisis.

The critics proposed a very different approach in the report of the majority group within the Meltzer commission:

"All resource transfers to countries that enjoy capital market access (as denoted by an investment grade international bond rating) or with a per capita income in excess of $4000, would be phased out over the next 5 years. Starting at $2500 (per capita income), official assistance would be limited. (Dollar values should be indexed). [For the record, indexation since 2000 would raise the above dollar figures to roughly $4500 and $2800, respectively, in late 2005 terms]."[11]

Meltzer's proposal to arbitrarily limit lending to countries with per capita incomes above $2800, and to apply a rigid phase out of all lending to countries with income per head of over $4500, would knock out or limit development support to most developing and transition countries in Latin America and Eastern Europe. It would convert the Bank from a strong development agency with a global reach into a much-shrunk body dealing primarily with Africa and a few low-income Asian countries.

Meltzer's addition of "market access" as a further reason for withdrawing eligibility to borrow would be an even more radical departure.[12] A borrower's access to private lending, as measured by agencies' credit ratings, does not reflect its level of development, so much as its prudence in borrowing and servicing its debts. India undoubtedly deserves credit for the policy reforms that recently lifted it to an "investment" rating. But with 850 million Indians (four in five of the population) surviving on less than $2 a day, one may question whether the international community truly wants its congratulatory card to India to read, as the critics would draft it, "You're on your own now!"

The heart of the matter?

The critics have concentrated their fire on the World Bank. But their central objections to IBRD lending to MICs apply with comparable logic to any official development lending to these countries—whether from regional banks, bilateral development agencies or wherever. Their real objection is evidently not to the specifics of the Bank's lending programs or its policy advice—subjects they barely begin to discuss. Nor have they seriously tried to prove the Bank less competent than its peers. Rather, the core of their case—even if generally camouflaged beneath the quibbling over this or that detail about the Bank—implies hostility to public development work in and of itself. Like left-wing activists who mobilize against McDonalds rather than its less-conspicuous competitors, the critics have identified the World Bank as the most visible symbol of public development assistance—and opposition to IBRD's work in the middle income countries as the thin edge of a larger ideological wedge.

Table I
The Middle Income Countries

IBRD Eligible Countries[1]	Protected Areas (Thousands of Hectares)[2]	CO_2 Emissions (Thousands of Metric Tons)[2]	Population[3]	% under $2/day[4]	Estimated Population under $2/day
Algeria	11,864	74,176	32,531,853	15.10	4,912,310
Antigua and Barbuda	0	359	68,722	NA	NA
Argentina	5,911	138,983	39,537,943	14.31	5,657,880
Azerbaijan	394	29,490	7,911,974	9.10	719,990
Barbados	0	1,334	279,254	NA	NA
Belarus	1,304	59,561	10,300,483	0.68	70,043
Belize	633	827	279,457	NA	NA
Bolivia	12,082	11,714	8,857,870	34.30	3,038,249
Bosnia and Herzegovina	27	14,269	4,025,476	NA	NA
Botswana	10,499	4,033	1,640,115	50.10	821,698
Brazil	32,866	327,858	186,112,794	22.43	41,745,100
Bulgaria	594	44,731	7,450,349	16.20	1,206,957
Chile	2,650	54,790	15,980,912	9.58	1,530,971
China	105,527	3,473,597	1,306,313,812	46.70	610,048,550
Colombia	9,786	63,998	42,954,279	22.56	9,690,485
Costa Rica	477	5,223	4,016,173	9.45	379,528
Croatia	339	19,191	4,495,904	0.53	23,828
Czech Republic	196	124,069	10,241,138	0.23	23,555
Dominica	10	76	69,029	NA	NA
Dominican Republic	1,113	19,887	8,950,034	0.76	68,020
Ecuador	2,308	20,705	13,363,593	36.09	4,822,921
Egypt, Arab Rep.	4,536	127,131	77,505,756	43.90	34,025,027
El Salvador	NA	6,598	6,704,932	58.02	3,890,202
Equatorial Guinea	455	716	535,881	NA	NA
Estonia	350	14,884	1,332,893	4.69	62,513
Fiji	16	701	893,354	NA	NA
Gabon	80	1,455	1,389,201	NA	NA
Grenada	NA	79	89,502	NA	NA
Guatemala	594	10,097	14,655,189	37.36	5,475,179
Hungary	821	56,850	10,006,835	1.52	152,104

Table I (continued)
The Middle Income Countries

IBRD Eligible Countries[1]	Protected Areas (Thousands of Hectares)[2]	CO_2 Emissions (Thousands of Metric Tons)[2]	Population[3]	% under $2/day[4]	Estimated Population under $2/day
India	15,291	1,007,979	1,080,264,388	79.90	863,131,246
Indonesia	8,607	286,027	241,973,879	52.42	126,842,707
Iran, Islamic Rep.	10,376	297,930	68,017,860	7.30	4,965,304
Iraq	1	78,507	26,074,906	NA	NA
Jamaica	0	10,320	2,731,832	13.30	363,334
Jordan	913	15,535	5,759,732	7.40	426,220
Kazakhstan	7,742	123,686	15,185,844	8.45	1,283,204
Korea, Republic of	350	470,020	48,422,644	1.00	484,226
Latvia	818	6,490	2,290,237	8.30	190,090
Lebanon	4	15,569	3,826,018	NA	NA
Libya	122	42,275	7,765,563	NA	NA
Lithuania	592	11,574	3,596,617	6.90	248,167
Macedonia, FYR	180	8,862	2,071,210	4.00	82,848
Malaysia	1,366	123,603	23,953,136	9.30	2,227,642
Marshall Islands	NA	NA	59,071	NA	NA
Mauritius	7	2,796	1,230,602	NA	NA
Mexico	1,205	385,075	106,202,903	24.30	25,807,305
Micronesia	5	NA	108,105	NA	NA
Morocco	326	33,236	32,725,847	14.30	4,679,796
Namibia	3,214	1,945	2,030,692	55.80	1,133,126
Pakistan	3,509	105,983	162,419,946	65.60	106,547,485
Palau	0	242	20,303	NA	NA
Panama	483	5,709	3,039,150	17.90	544,008
Papua New Guinea	7	2,445	5,545,268	NA	NA
Paraguay	1,391	3,659	6,347,884	30.29	1,922,774
Peru	4,010	28,194	27,925,628	37.71	10,530,754
Philippines	1,513	75,299	87,857,973	47.48	41,714,966
Poland	3,417	303,777	38,635,144	1.18	455,895
Romania	476	90,729	22,329,977	20.50	4,577,645

Table I (continued)
The Middle Income Countries

IBRD Eligible Countries[1]	Protected Areas (Thousands of Hectares)[2]	CO$_2$ Emissions (Thousands of Metric Tons)[2]	Population[3]	% under $2/day[4]	Estimated Population under $2/day
Russian Federation	90,223	1,540,365	143,420,309	23.80	34,134,034
Serbia and Montenegro	327	44,355	10,829,175	NA	NA
Seychelles	4	224	81,188	NA	NA
Slovak Republic	357	36,927	5,431,363	2.40	130,353
South Africa	6,461	344,590	44,344,136	34.07	15,108,047
St. Lucia	2	446	166,312	NA	NA
St. Vincent and the Grenadines	4	165	117,534	NA	NA
Suriname	1,846	2,244	438,144	NA	NA
Swaziland	35	388	1,173,900	22.55	264,714
Syrian Arab Republic	NA	51,347	18,448,752	NA	NA
Thailand	6,516	171,697	65,444,371	32.50	21,269,421
Trinidad and Tobago	24	18,090	1,088,644	39.00	424,571
Tunisia	28	20,179	10,074,951	10.00	1,007,495
Turkey	571	223,862	69,660,559	10.30	7,175,038
Turkmeni-stan	1,883	34,584	4,952,081	44.00	2,178,916
Ukraine	1,937	348,357	47,425,336	45.70	21,673,379
Uruguay	30	6,409	3,415,920	1.00	34,159
Uzbekistan	2,050	121,045	26,851,195	44.20	11,868,228
Venezuela, RB	31,358	136,686	25,275,281	32.00	8,088,090
Zimbabwe	3,103	14,098	12,746,990	64.20	8,183,568
MIC Totals	**418,112**	**11,360,906**	**4,338,293,207**		**2,058,063,861**
World Totals	**806,722**	**23,895,742**	**6,482,257,297**		**2,706,036,650**
% of World Total	**51.83**	**47.54**	**66.93**		**76.05**

Table I (continued)
The Middle Income Countries

[1]Countries are those eligible to borrow from the IBRD as of
December, 2005.
[2]Source: World Resources Institute EarthTrends
(http://earthtrends.wri.org/).
[3]Source: United Nations World Population Prospects Database
(http://esa.un.org/unpp/).
[4]Source: World Bank/WDI, supplemented by PovCalNet.

Notes

1. The author is grateful for the invaluable contribution of Anthony Ody to the overall preparation of this chapter, and for research assistance from William Gee.

2. The term "middle-income countries" refers here to those eligible to borrow from the World Bank's non-concessional IBRD (International Bank for Reconstruction and Development) window, which lends at interest rates slightly above the World Bank's own cost of borrowing in the international capital markets. By contrast, "low income countries" mostly borrow from the Bank's concessional IDA (International Development Association) window at substantially softer terms, with the flows funded largely from periodic "replenishments" voted by the Bank's more affluent shareholder countries (supplemented by internal transfers from IBRD earnings). A few countries borrow simultaneously from IDA and IBRD: these "blend" countries are for most purposes counted within the "middle income" classification.

3. Allan H. Meltzer, chairman, *Report of the International Financial Institutions Advisory Commission* (Washington, D.C., 2000), available at http://www.house.gov/jec/imf/ifiac.htm.

4. "Charting a Way Ahead: the Results Agenda" Address to the 2005 Annual Meetings by Paul Wolfowitz. September 24, 2005. World Bank.

5. World Bank News Release No. 2006/205/S (December 13, 2005).

6. The strategic importance of the middle income countries for the realization of many international goals—and for donor countries supporting these goals—are

addressed in greater detail in a later section of the chapter.

7. Data for fiscal year 2006, released just before publication of this volume, confirmed the continued recovery of IBRD approvals—up another 4 percent above fiscal 2005, to the highest level in seven years ($14.1 billion). Data available at: http://web.worldbank.org/WBSITE/EXTERNAL/NEWS/0,,contentMDK:21016240~pagePK:64257043~piPK:437376~theSitePK:4607,00.html.

8. See especially *The Role of the Multilateral Development Banks in Emerging Market Economies*, the report of a commission co-chaired by José Angel Gurria and Paul Volcker (Washington, D. C.: Carnegie Endowment for International Peace, 2001), and *The Hardest Job in the World: Five Crucial Tasks for the New President of the World Bank*, report of a Center for Global Development working group co-chaired by Nancy Birdsall and Devesh Kapur, in this volume.

9. See *The Hardest Job in the World*, Birdsall and Kapur (2006) for more.

10. *The World Bank Annual Report 2005*, (Washington, D. C.: The World Bank, 2005).

11. Meltzer, *Report of the International Financial Institutions Advisory Commission*.

12. Note, too, that while the commission's text refers only to cutting off countries with "investment grade," some of Prof. Lerrick's comments in the present debate implicitly question the rationale for support even to countries with below-investment grade ratings (more commonly known as "junk" ratings).

The Missing Mandate: Global Public Goods

by Michael Kremer

This note discusses the potential role of the World Bank in providing global public goods. From an economic point of view, global public goods are those for which a large share of the benefit cannot be contained within a single country. For instance, a country that establishes a policy to reduce carbon emissions to prevent global warming does not just benefit itself but helps all countries that would be hurt by global warming. Likewise, a successful campaign to eradicate polio would not only improve health in those countries where the disease persists, but would also save other governments hundreds of millions of dollars a year in avoided immunization costs.

It's worth noting that there is a continuum in the extent to which the benefits of goods spill over across borders. Reductions in carbon emissions or efforts to eradicate polio are at one end of the continuum, while efforts to, for example, expand the use of nets to fight malaria are at the other, since most epidemiological models would suggest that the great majority of the benefits of net programs fall within a country, although theoretically there might be some reduction in transmission of disease to the neighboring countries. (As this example illustrates, not every worthwhile investment is a global public good, and the international community should not feel that every activity undertaken by international organizations needs to be justified as falling under this rubric.)

The full value of global public goods is not reflected in an individual country's own cost-benefit analysis. As such, governments often have inadequate incentives to devote their own resources to these programs.

Michael Kremer, Harvard University and Center for Global Development
Michael Kremer is professor of economics at Harvard University, senior fellow at the Brookings Institution, and non-resident fellow at the Center for Global Development. Kremer serves as associate editor of the *Journal of Development Economics* and the *Quarterly Journal of Economics*. He is an expert on AIDS and infectious diseases in developing countries, economics of developing countries, education and development, and mechanisms for encouraging research and development.

International organizations such as the World Bank fill this void by supporting global public goods. Of course some global public goods, such as development of improved algorithms for matching kidney donors to patients, would benefit primarily rich countries. For equity reasons, the World Bank may want to focus on those global public goods for which a large share of the benefit goes to poor countries.

When the Bank was limited to providing loans to governments, the Bank's instruments for promoting global public goods were likewise restricted. It is difficult for the World Bank to ask a country to repay any substantial part of a loan if the benefits are primarily for other countries. Because it now can offer grants, the Bank has the potential to do much more to promote global public goods that benefit the poor. It may make sense for the Bank to set up a funding mechanism for these global public goods that is separate from IDA.

In particular, the Bank might consider a separate funding mechanism that could make investments in the following global public goods: 1) technologies for the poor, 2) developing knowledge about what works in public policy, 3) a road network for Africa, and 4) creating incentives for countries to house and care for refugees.

Technologies for the Poor
The development of certain health and agricultural technologies, such as a schistosomiasis vaccine or improved cassava varieties, would affect the lives of people in many developing countries. While private companies are often motivated to develop new technologies based on a combination of up-front public funding as well as the prospect of a market, markets for these technologies either do not exist or function poorly.

The Bank can help overcome these hurdles in two ways. First, it can use its funds to support research. In the past the Bank has used part of its profits to support the development of agricultural technologies through institutions like the CGIAR system. The Bank could expand its support of these activities and of the development of health technologies as well.

The second approach would be for the Bank to use its resources to create a market for the needed products and thus create incentives for private firms to invest in these technologies. In particular, the Bank could make a commitment to extend loans or grants to help countries finance the purchase of certain goods, like the purchase of a schistosomiasis vaccine.[1]

Moreover, if the Bank had a separate financing mechanism devoted specifically to supporting global public goods, it could do much more than lend money to countries to buy vaccines. The Bank could also offer up-front to devote its resources to the creation of new vaccines, through an Advance Market commitment for example.

Developing Knowledge on Public Policy

A second global public good that targets poor countries is the development of a solid knowledge base on the impact of various public policies in these settings.

Oportunidades, the conditional cash transfer program in Mexico formerly known as PROGRESA, is a prime example of the benefits of combining policy innovation with rigorous evaluation to determine their impact. Mexico developed a very sophisticated evaluation mechanism for Oportunidades, which included randomizing the order in which the program was phased in across villages. The high quality evaluation techniques created a reliable evidence base that has not only helped lead Mexico to preserve and expand the program, but also led other countries to adopt similar programs. (The IDB played a role in this, and the Bank has played a role in expanding this type of program.)

The Bank could support countries interested in testing new approaches through an innovation and evaluation fund. Through such a fund, the Bank could make resources available, with a large grant element, to countries that are willing to subject programs of potential interest to other countries to a rigorous evaluation, including randomization of the order of phase-in.

African Road Network

Support for an African road network would provide a regional public good to one of the poorest areas in the world. (Since there are other financial institutions that specifically serve this region, some have argued the Bank follow the subsidiarity principle by funding or offering co-financing to those institutions, such as the African Development Bank.)

If the Bank were to consider such a program, it would be critical to provide for a continued role of international institutions in preservation and maintenance of the road, including preventing the overloading of trucks, which damages roads. In the absence of such an international role, there may not be sufficient incentive to prevent road damage from heavy trucks since much of the cost of that kind of road deterioration would be shared with neighboring countries.[2]

Support for Refugees

More speculatively, support for refugees can be considered an international public good. Each country would rather that another accept refugees. This is one justification for the international treaties which require signatories to accept political refugees. Yet the current system creates a number of problems.

Maintaining refugees in camps concentrates them in a particular area, making it harder for them to work in the normal economy, and leaving them plenty of time and incentive to engage in politics, including violent political activities. We have seen this most recently with Rwandan refugees in Congo. We also saw it in Afghanistan, and with the Palestinians.

In some instances, powerful political actors may have political motivations for keeping refugees in camps. For instance, some may have felt that in order to keep pressure on Israel, it was strategically useful to have Palestinians in refugee camps rather than dispersed and resettled throughout the Arab world. On the other hand, there are certainly some cases—the Hutu militias and other refugees that fled to Congo might be a good example—in which there is no strong international political force which is lobbying for refugees to be maintained in camps, and there might be prospects for reform.

One way the Bank might assist in such situations would be to support countries, especially non-neighboring countries, that are willing to take in refugees and to let them integrate into their society. For example, if the World Bank had a mandate in this area, it could have provided assistance to countries that were willing to take in refugees on condition that they would allow them to settle freely. For example, there could have been assistance to countries like Kenya if they accepted Rwandan refugees. Had this occurred, it is possible the invasion of Congo and the terrible war there could have been avoided.

Conclusion

Global public goods present a problem to the international community. Because the returns on an investment in these goods are shared around the world, individual countries rarely have the incentive to devote their own resources to providing them. The World Bank, armed now with grant instruments in addition to loans, is in a unique position to support the creation and maintenance of these goods. It would be appropriate for the Bank to focus on the

Notes

1. See Michael Kremer and Rachel Glennerster, *Strong Medicine: Creating Incentives for Pharmaceutical Research on Neglected Diseases*, (Princeton, New Jersey: Princeton University Press, 2004); Owen Barder, Michael Kremer and Ruth Levine, *Making Markets for Vaccines: Ideas to Action*, (Washington D.C.: Center for Global Development, 2005); Michael Kremer and Rachel Glennerster, "A World Bank Vaccine Commitment," Brookings Institution Policy Brief #57 (May 2000), http://www.brookings.edu/comm/policybriefs/pb57.htm.
2. See Nancy Birdsall, "Underfunded Regionalism in the Developing World," in *The New Public Finance: Responding to Global Challenges*, eds. Inge Kaul and Pedro Conceição, (Oxford: Oxford University Press, 2006).

The "Knowledge" Bank

by Devesh Kapur

I deas have always been a core trait of the Bank. Indeed, if the Bank was simply a financial intermediary, it would barely need a tenth of its staff.[1] The money was seen as the lubricant to move the main product—ideas on what to do, how to do it, who should do it and for whom. In its early decades, this importance of ideas was implicit. The source of ideas was the knowledge embedded in its experienced personnel and the transmission mechanism was the project mode. Since the 1970s, however, the Bank became more self-conscious about the importance of knowledge, both as an imprimatur institution as well as a producer of knowledge. And in more recent years, the relative decline in the importance of the Bank's financial role (especially in emerging markets), in part the result of the high transactions costs of borrowing from the Bank, has led to a greater stress on its role as a "knowledge" intermediary rather than just (or even primarily) as a financial intermediary. However, lending has been the principal mechanism for knowledge transfer, and any stagnation or decline in lending is likely to adversely impact knowledge transfer as well.

The World Bank's extensive (and expensive) commitment to the production and dissemination of knowledge has led to substantial critical analysis of the Bank's "knowledge" activities. Yet there is an analytical vacuum on key issues that bear on the subject, be it the optimal quantum of budgetary resources allocated to this area, the distribution of those resources among different research activities, between generation and diffusion, or the optimal institutional mechanisms to generate and transmit the research, whether in-house or externally.

***Devesh Kapur, University of Pennsylvania and
the Center for Global Development***
Devesh Kapur holds the Madan Lal Sobti Professorship for the Study of Contemporary India and is the Director of the Center for the Advanced Study of India at the University of Pennsylvania. He is also a non-resident fellow at the Center for Global Development. His recent publications include *Give Us Your Best and Brightest: The Global Hunt for Talent and Its Impact on the Developing World* (Center for Global Development, 2005) and *Public Institutions in India: Performance and Design* (Oxford University Press, 2005).

Consider for instance the following hypothetical questions:

1. If the Bank's overall budget was cut by a third and the resulting savings (more than half billion annually) were put into research in those diseases, crops and energy technologies that are sui generis to poor countries, would the global welfare of the poor improve or decline?

2. If the Bank were to cut its "Analytical and Advisory Activities" (AAA) expenditures (from its estimated $600 million in 2005), shifting its focus from the social sciences to funding research in the health sciences, would the global welfare of the poor increase or decline?

3. If the Bank's research activities were more akin to a National Science Foundation (NSF) type funding activity, rather than in-house research, would LDCs gain or lose?

4. If the Bank were to reallocate part of its large transfers from net income (about $600 million annually over the past few years) to create endowments for centers of learning in LDCs, would those countries be better off?

This paper argues that the World Bank should give greater emphasis to financing rather than producing research, in particular, financing developing country research institutions. Despite the modest quality of the latter, such a shift is likely to be more effective in changing national policies and in nurturing implementation. It will also contribute to long-run institution building (at a minimum, by not reinforcing the brain drain).

Although a large array of studies has demonstrated the high rates of social return in publicly funded research, this in itself does not provide any guidance either on which areas to finance investment in, nor the precise mechanism to undertake this task.[2] High average values for publicly funded research are of little use in deciding whether to increase (or decrease) funding for public research, or in choosing the mechanism that would yield the best results (resource allocation decisions require some sense of marginal rather than average rates of return). Moreover, there is no analytical framework that would help answer whether the World Bank should conduct research in-house, outsource it by funding universities or research centers (and if so, create country—or sector-specific centers), promote joint research ventures (including exchange of personnel), or build research networks (such as the Global Development Network).

The dilemmas are compounded by the reality that research capabilities are located in the North while many of the issue areas, with the highest rates of social return to public investments in research, are in resource-poor countries. Furthermore, even if the World Bank were to outsource its research and fund more research, what mechanisms should it follow? For instance, in areas where research is undersupplied because of severe market failures—such as tropical diseases, where pharmaceutical firms do not invest fearing that were they to actually develop a product, they would face severe public pressure to sell the product at a price that would not justify the initial investment—a novel mechanism that has been proposed is for public agencies to finance "tournaments" with a prize guaranteed to any entity that meets predetermined specifications at a certain price.[3] Although such an approach would not build developing countries' own capabilities, it might be warranted in areas where delay has high human costs.

The stakes are different, however, in policy research, the core focus of the Bank's AAA. The background of Bank researchers creates strong incentives to give pride of place to *propositional* knowledge—the search for "universal" laws of development from the frontiers of academia—and using that to generate *prescriptive* knowledge. LDC-based researchers are seldom, if ever, represented in the former. Does that matter? There are several good reasons why concerns on this score may not be warranted. For one, there are typically participants from developing countries in conferences focusing on propositional knowledge. It just so happens that their institutional base is in industrialized countries (typically the United States). Second, the idea that one's analytical position is an isomorphic reflection of one's nationality and/or geographical base is rather specious. Third, one could argue that the Bank should only be drawing on the best talent to understand difficult issues, and if it happens that the talent is based in North America, so be it. Fourth, the fears of a lack of diversity are misplaced, given the vigorous debates and differences that are integral to academic and intellectual cultures. And finally, the skewed participation may simply reflect the realities of the global production of knowledge, in which LDCs themselves have played a not insignificant role by running their own universities and knowledge production systems to the ground.

However, there are reasons for unease as well. Intellectual networks can be double-edged. While they reduce selection costs and serve as reputational mechanisms, they can also be prone to a form of "crony intellectualism." This inherent tendency to inbreeding has negative consequences for intellectual advancement. Researchers, like other societal groups, also have interests. And research involvement with the World Bank has substantial payoffs, from research funding to access to data and visibility. Moreover, the very nature of academia means that academic researchers (in the social sciences) are not accountable for the consequence in the sense that their work responds to professional incentives, not to its development payoffs. These professional incentives place a large positive premium in academic papers on the novelty of ideas, methodological innovation, generalizability and parsimonious explanations. Detailed country and sector knowledge, an acknowledgement that the ideas may be sensible but not especially novel, that uncertainty and complexity rather than parsimony are perhaps the ground reality, are all poor country-cousins of research that purports to find universal truths. The mainline prestigious journals usually give short shrift to articles with micro-data painstakingly collected in a LDC. These journals act as gatekeepers of knowledge as well as reputation but are important markers for the Bank on the who, how and what dominates its research agenda. For the most part, this service is positive, given the concentration of talent in these institutions. But the fact is that unless a researcher is part of this circuit, she is marginalized.

This is also an important reason why the Bank's knowledge activities have underemphasized the crucial long-term contributions of its didactic and educational role. The very fact that the vast majority of the Bank's work on poverty is in English, a language understood by almost none of world's poor, indicates the low status assigned to this role, and cannot be understood without reference both to the internal incentives and external networks of

Bank staff which skew the priorities of research staff in these institutions. The professional payoffs of delivering a paper on Africa are substantially greater in Cambridge, Massachusetts, than in Ouagadougou. In turn that means that the questions and methodologies will be geared to the priorities of the former, even though the latter has more at stake. Growth regressions have undoubtedly helped in the growth of researchers, but have they contributed to the growth of poor countries themselves? The search for universality offers little by way of prescriptive knowledge in a particular situation. Yes, institutions matter, but anyone examining the first few decades of the Bank would not view this insight as a Eureka moment. In the end, such prospective knowledge offers little insight into prescriptive knowledge. Of the scores of institutions that matter, which institution is most critical in which country at any specific period of time cannot get around the need for its having a deeply textured knowledge of the circumstances of the country itself. And it offers even less by way of guidance to the most glaring weaknesses of poor countries: *how* to build these institutions and *who* would do so.

The virtual absence of researchers based in developing countries in the more prestigious development conferences cannot be attributed simply to exclusionary networks. Given the outpouring of reports on key global debates involving the World Bank, networks and reputation are critical screening mechanisms. On both counts, a base in a developing country virtually ensures extinction. The developing countries—especially the larger ones—have much to answer for themselves, having failed to develop and maintain reputational institutions in the social sciences.[5] The poor quality of developing country academic institutions in the social sciences has led the Bank to not only draw its research staff from U.S. universities in particular (which then creates research networks between the staff and faculty in those universities), but when these institutions want to train and support developing country students or send their own staff for training, it is invariably again at U.S. universities.[6] Given the outstanding quality of the latter, the short-run compulsions of the Bretton Woods institutions are quite understandable, but their long-term consequences are inimical. These practices have strengthened already strong research institutions in the U.S. while further weakening developing country institutions—creating conditions for perpetuating the practice. The process has generated a vicious circle with results that are in line with models of statistical discrimination. The more the World Bank and the IMF in effect discriminate against researchers from LDCs, the more the incentive of these researchers to migrate out of the countries either to these institutions themselves or to developed countries where their credibility is enhanced by their association with a developed country institution, furthering the decline of LDC research institutions.

It is not that there are no universal "truths" about development, but rather that they make the Bank a prisoner as often as they liberate the institution from past mistakes. Consequently, the Bank's knowledge activities have been more captive to the fads and fashions of academia, moving from one big idea to the next, rather than knowledge activities that might be most helpful to its borrowers. Fig. 1 is a schematic representation of these cycles, where new ideas lead to new projects and programs, with recruitment and expertise usually lagging. As time passes, evaluations and feedback usually paint a more somber picture, requiring course correction. But even as the knowledge resulting from learning-by-doing begins to get accumulated, a form of intellectual *ennui* sets in and a new set of ideas (often precipitated by a change in guard at the top), begins a new cycle. From rural development in the 1970s to structural adjustment in the 1980s to institutional changes such as judicial reforms in the 1990s, much new knowledge has been learnt in the Bank—and forgotten as it is crowded out by new ideas and agendas.

Consequently, the substantial resources devoted by the Bank to self-evaluation have had limited effects—the sum being considerably less than its parts. The evaluation methodology has been questioned, in particular, on whether in the absence of randomized trials, lessons from these evaluations can be meaningfully extrapolated. While a valid criticism, the growing fashion for randomized trials glosses over the reality that while providing valuable insights for a particular context, they too have weaknesses in the lessons they provide for similar projects but in different contexts. The more troubling weaknesses are that the tacit knowledge born of experience has become a premium in the institution as the average experience of Bank staff has fallen sharply. While new blood is always critical, periodic reorganizations and perennial transfers have ensured that loud displays of innovation are often old wine (if not old vinegar) in new bottles, born more of inexperience than perspicacity. But in the end, even the best of evaluation techniques and self-knowledge are at the mercy of the willingness and ability of the Bank's top echelons to be open-minded and guided by empirical knowledge. That in turn is a function of the Bank's governance.

As a result, a half century into "development," developing countries still seem incapable of thinking for themselves on issues (to put it crudely) critical to their own welfare, at least as measured by the lack of meaningful contributions that would find a place at the high seats of social science research. What has the Bank done in the last half-century to build institutions in developing countries that could help them think for themselves?

For the most part, the answer is "not much." Even as MNCs increasingly have diversified the geographical location of research activities, research is still relatively centralized in the Bretton Woods institutions—and to the extent that ideas shape agendas, centralized control of research is an excellent unobtrusive approach to set the agenda. Large salary differentials offered by these institutions and developing country research institutions

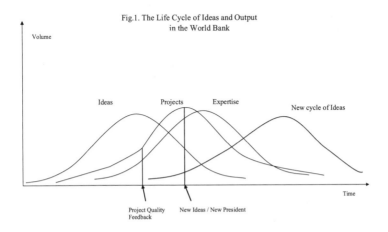

Fig.1. The Life Cycle of Ideas and Output
in the World Bank

Volume

Ideas   Projects   Expertise   New cycle of Ideas

Time

Project Quality   New Ideas / New President
Feedback

(with the exception of some Latin American countries) means that they often draw out limited talent in developing countries. Moreover, for nearly two decades the Bank has been chary of supporting institutions of higher learning, directing resources to primary and secondary education and justifying this shift both on equity and efficiency grounds. Foundations have also joined the bandwagon against supporting research institutions in developing countries on the grounds that they were elitist and that instead, "grass-roots" institutions needed more support. In both cases there was more than ample justification for the shift—but in the process, Bank (and the Foundations) have thrown the baby out with the bathwater. It has meant that developing country researchers are by and large restricted to data collection and country-specific applied work, not only incapable of contributing anything meaningful to agenda setting debates ranging from global financial architecture to second generation reforms, but remaining dependent on continuing and often second-rate technical assistance that is also very expensive.

Should the Bank move from a producer to a financier of knowledge?

As an intergovernmental organization, the World Bank's knowledge activities will always be subject to pressures from members. If, in the 1980s, debt and corruption were a no-mans land, in recent years intellectual property rights, capital account liberalization and genetically modified crops are examples of issue areas that the Bank has had to tiptoe around. If the value of the Bank's research as a global public good is undermined by its perceived lack of independence, other factors would appear to strengthen the case of the Bank moving from a producer of research to a financier of research.

First, there are substantial opportunity costs. It should be emphasized that in-house knowledge-related activities at the Bank are expensive, even when compared to U.S. universities, let alone LDCs. Second, there are important strategic benefits of publicly funded research for developing countries, particularly the creation of capabilities, through the vital links between research and the supply of skilled graduates. To put it differently, the process of research creates capabilities that allow for better consumption or use of knowledge. Additionally, public funding of research in different environments plays an important role in the creation of diverse options. The domination of a narrow set of institutions (reflecting in part their outstanding quality) has several undesirable consequences. It skews the questions, methodologies and other priorities of research. As a result, those directly affected by the policies of the institutions are underrepresented in setting the research and policy agenda. Furthermore, it narrows the diversity of views, which, given limited knowledge and the possibility of wrong advice, could amplify risk in the international system. The importance of diversity is particularly important in the context of an uncertain future.[7] Moreover, diversity may matter in and of itself on the grounds that there should be at least a minimum degree of participation by those likely to be affected by the actions resulting from ideas emanating from these institutions. Diversity may also be important for its instrumentality—it diversifies risk, a not unimportant criterion, given limited knowledge and the consequences of misplaced advice.

The rhetoric of the Word Bank and IMF on institutions notwithstanding, they have been tepid in supporting initiatives to develop knowledge-producing institutional capacity in LDCs, although over the last decade the World Bank has made some efforts to support regional research centers.[8] Its support for the Global Development Network (GDN, which has now been spun off as an independent entity) is an interesting innovation aimed at linking researchers and policy institutes involved in the field of development. The network also aims at skill and reputation building. This is a commendable effort, although it is too early to gauge its impact. However, even the GDN is unlikely to address the problem of how developing country researchers can overcome the high reputational barriers that exist on research and policies related to systemic issues. That requires a receptivity and openness in these institutions themselves, which is structurally difficult. Virtually all the links in the research Web sites of the Bank and Fund are to researchers in developed countries, a reflection of the modest quality of research from LDCs but also an indication of the personal networks of research staff in these institutions.

Consequently, it would appear that all factors, from operating costs to opportunity costs (using the resources to build capabilities in LDCs), would seem to support a serious reconsideration of the allocation of AAA-related resources by the World Bank. But not surprisingly, there are countervailing factors as well. First, conducting in-house research has operational externalities for the Bank. The possibility of being able to undertake research at the Bank attracts higher quality personnel (especially economists) who then contribute positively to the operations side of the Bank. Moreover, what is true of developing countries is also true of the Bank: in-house research capabilities increase the ability to sift through the copious volumes of new knowledge and ideas and make better judgments in separating the wheat from the chaff. Second, and contrary to popular impressions, it is easier for the Bank to restructure its internal AAA, than restructure its support to external research institutions.[9]

But even if the World Bank were to finance knowledge activities in LDCs to a greater degree, a different set of dilemmas arises—should the activities be focused on knowledge activities that are more national or global? While the case for the latter seems evident, in some issue areas the quest for supplying knowledge-related public goods at the global level may be amplifying the deficit at the national level. Agricultural research is a case in point. According to one estimate, even in the 1980s, while nearly a third of the hundreds of agricultural researchers who routinely attended the CGIAR's annual "Centers' Week" meetings at the World Bank were originally from LDCs, more recently only about one in 20 were still actually affiliated with LDC national research institutes or universities. With donors viewing the building of higher education and research capacity in LDCs as "elitist," research as a public good is seen to be better supplied at the global rather than the national level. However, it may well be the case that in areas ranging from agricultural to economics research, LDC researchers faced with rewards that are much greater in international rather than national research organizations, gravitate toward the former. As a result, while the supply of global public goods (in the form of research in agriculture and economics) is reasonably adequate, public goods deficits at the national level, involving the production of country-specific knowledge, may be increasing.

Conclusion

There is no development institution that has devoted as many resources to knowledge-related activities as the

World Bank. It is therefore surprising that the Bank has had little appetite to develop a rigorous framework that at a minimum analyzes the opportunity costs of these substantial knowledge-related expenditures. Admittedly the task would be analytically difficult, but there are few incentives within the institution to do so. Arguably, if even a tenth of this expenditure was instead redirected at creating endowments for knowledge-producing centers in developing countries, it is at least an open question if the welfare of those societies may not be higher. It may help LDCs to think for themselves—and take responsibility for the actions resulting from their ideas—rather than be the perennial objects of received wisdom.

Notes

1. As is the case with the European Investment Bank, whose loan portfolio has been larger than the Bank but which is otherwise a much smaller institution.

2. See, for instance, A.J. Salter and B.R. Martin, "The economic benefits of publicly funded research: a critical review." *Research Policy* 30 (2001): 509–532.

3. Of course the prize must be large enough to be attractive for organizations to undertake the investments. For an application to vaccines, see Michael Kremer, "Creating Markets for New Vaccines—Part I: Rationale, Part II: Design Issues," *Innovation Policy and the Economy*, Vol. 1 (2000): 35–118.

4. Pranab Bardhan, "Journal Publication in Economics: A View from the Periphery," *The Economic Journal* 113 (2003): F332-F337.

5. The case of India is illustrative. In the 1990s, of the 2,312 articles in the top five journals in economics (AER, EJ, JPE, QJE and Review of Economic Studies), 138 were by Indians outside India and just seven were from Indians in India—a factor of 20!

6. At the beginning of the 1990s, 80 percent of the research staff at the World Bank had graduate degrees from U.S. and U.K. institutions (nearly two-thirds from the U.S.). While similar data from the IMF is unavailable,

it is unlikely to be less. Since then, widening quality differences between U.S. and developing country academic institutions are likely to have increased the skewedness. See Nicholas Stern, "The World Bank as Intellectual Actor," Table 18-12-6, in Devesh Kapur, John Lewis and Richard Webb, *The World Bank: Its First Half Century* (Washington, D.C.: The Brookings Institution, 1997).

7. Andrew Stirling, "On the Economics and Analysis of Diversity." SPRU Working Papers, University of Sussex, Brighton (1998).

8. These include the Africa Economic Research Consortium (AERC) and the Joint Vienna Institute (cosponsored with the BIS, the EBRD, the IMF and the OECD). But the output of these institutions is not geared to addressing systemic issues—as attested by the fact that their work is rarely cited by the sponsoring institutions themselves. The IDB has been more creative in this regard. It has been coordinating the Latin American Research Network, created in 1991, and funds leading research centers in the region to conduct research on economic and social issues in Latin America and the Caribbean. The research topics are determined through consultation with IDB and external professionals.

9. This is exemplified by the Bank's large financial support over more than three decades to the CGIAR system. There can be little doubt that certain centers need to be closed down and the limited resources shifted to others, but for political economy reasons this has been stymied, leading to a sub-optimal allocation of resources within the CGIAR system.

Evaluations and Aid Effectiveness

by Pierre Jacquet[1]

All bilateral and multilateral development institutions devote important resources to evaluating their operations. This activity is generally assigned to a dedicated unit placed outside the purview of the operational sphere so as to protect it from any vested interests; it is also often conducted in partnership with independent experts. Although they account for only a tiny proportion of public budgets, bilateral official development aid institutions probably even stand several steps ahead of many public administrations in thus contributing to the evaluation of public policies.[2] This brief paper, based on the experience of a bilateral development agency, claims that evaluations in fact fulfill several distinct, albeit related, valuable functions and that it is worthwhile to address each of them for their own sake as methods and organization need to be tailored accordingly. These are layman observations, however, that do not aim at constituting a "theory" of evaluations, but simply at providing some perspectives about an old but increasingly important function or set of functions in development institutions.

This paper does not primarily address the working of the World Bank Independent Evaluations Group (IEG, formerly OED—Operations Evaluation Department). I believe, however, that bilateral and multilateral development institutions all face similar challenges and should exchange more on their evaluation approaches and practices in order to improve on these practices and set common standards through a careful benchmarking process. Indeed, the description of IEG's evaluation tools and approaches[3] cover much of what I describe below as full-fledged "evaluation", even though I propose here

Pierre Jacquet, Agence Française de Développement
Pierre Jacquet has been executive director (in charge of strategy) and chief economist at Agence Française de Développement (the French Development Agency) since 2002. He was formerly deputy director of the French Institute of International Relations in Paris and chief editor of its quarterly review Politique Etrangère. He is professor of international economics and chairman of the Department of Economics and Social Sciences at Ecole nationale des ponts et chaussées. Between 1997 and 2006 he was a member of the Conseil d'Analyse Economique, an independent advisory panel created by the French Prime Minister.

a much more explicit separation between the various functions that I identify. In analyzing these functions, I also try to highlight some organizational consequences. Not everything needs to be "independent" or conducted outside the operational sphere. And, insofar as scientific impact evaluation is concerned, there is a powerful case for some form of coordination among development institutions.[4]

1. Current evaluations: a multi-purpose activity

While there is a welcome attention currently given to the development of scientific impact evaluations geared to seriously assessing the actual impact of ODA financed operations on development, two related observations stand out from the experience of development institutions: first, not much has been done in terms of conducting genuine scientific development impact measurements so far; second, this is in fact not what most development institutions call "evaluation" in the first place. Yet, existing evaluation units play important roles that it is worthwhile to recognize and strengthen. They typically simultaneously fulfill three useful, different, functions, while admittedly not serving other, useful purposes that do belong to evaluation and that are in short supply in the international community of donors.

Building knowledge on processes and institutions

The first role is a cognitive role of building operational knowledge of processes and practices within a development institution and about how they interact with practices, behaviors and institutions on the receiving side. Additionally, evaluations build knowledge about the countries in which donors operate, their societies, their institutions, their needs, the quality of their governance. In short, they contribute to an empirical field knowledge that helps staff build field experience and become seasoned to the intricacies and complexity of development aid. This aspect of "evaluations" is important for the institution and needs to be conducted in-house because it is part of a necessary process of self-knowledge and self-education. It is also key to improving practices. Critiques comparing that process with scientific impact evaluation are based on a confusion of roles. What such evaluations do amounts to capitalizing on the existing experience and creating transmissible knowledge from experience. They inform on processes and on the interaction between donor processes, practices and behaviors and institutions on the receiving side. They also point to shortcomings that can be remedied in subsequent operations. They can also be complementary to impact evaluations to the extent that they inform on why observed results may have been achieved.

A key aspect of evaluations, insofar as this first role is concerned, relates to the feedback process through which the results from these evaluations, however conducted, will inspire new actions. Substantial improvement needs to take place on feedback and retroaction, even though these dimensions have been recognized for a long time and have often led to substantial quality improvement. How to make feedback more systematic should be a top management priority. There is a natural tendency to focus on the "production of knowledge" aspect of evaluations rather than on how to use that knowledge in daily operations. Insufficient time and resources are devoted to that process and the structure of incentives is more favorable to conducting evaluations than to learning from them in the operational process. Indeed, a key to "results-based management" should not be as much about designing success, a rather elusive goal, as about learning from failures. This is certainly an area in which much progress needs to be achieved. A former United Nations Food and Agriculture Organization (FAO) officer for example described in his book[5] how it took ten years for the FAO to abandon its recommendation that farmers use centralized storage facilities and villages establish cereal banks despite a record from evaluations that such centralization was inefficient and not viable.

While it is important, as we argue below, to add other dimensions to evaluations, it is also crucial to devote more time and resources to the feedback loop through which knowledge helps improve overall quality. This does not apply only to knowledge built through evaluations. An important aspect of quality management hinges on the ability of any institution to use all relevant knowledge in shaping its actions. Good practices must therefore ensure that decision processes do take into account results from past evaluations, but also current knowledge existing outside the institution and that needs to be identified and collected. Informing decision processes through these various channels is a priority.[6] A major difficulty, however, hinges on what is, or is not, relevant when taking a decision on whether to finance an operation, given the differences between past and current operations in terms of overall political, institutional, economic, social and technical environment.

Monitoring quality

Evaluations also fulfill an important monitoring role, that can be part and parcel of the practice of evaluations described in the preceding section, but that is of a different conceptual nature. It amounts to checking observed results against ex-ante expected ones and to monitoring the execution of operations: What was the objective of the program or project, was the money used for what it was supposed to, did it reach the intended beneficiaries, what was the time schedule for disbursements, how to explain any difference between actual versus expected results, and so on. This is an exercise in conformity and based on identifying good operational practices and on monitoring these practices. While the cognitive role alluded to above is best achieved through retrospective evaluations, quality needs to be monitored during execution and up to the end of any given operation.

As such, monitoring needs to be conducted within the operational sphere because this is where the relevant information is to be collected. Regular auditing must check that appropriate good practices and procedures have been followed. Monitoring also supplies useful information for the kind of evaluations that was mentioned in the preceding section. Here also, feedback, as a way to improve management, is an important dimension. It is central to quality management and control. Monitoring is thus an important instrument for top management.

External Accountability

As official development assistance deals with taxpayers' money, organizing accountability is of course a central task. There is, however, a necessary distinction to make between accountability and judgment. Development institutions are liable to provide an assessment of what they do and to communicate it to the outside. Accountability should amount to making all information available to the outside and let outsiders judge from that information and from their own perspective whether institutions make a good use of public money or not.

This aspect of evaluation systems, however, is open to challenge. There is an inherent conflict between the internal and external uses of information produced by evaluations. While the institution itself needs to learn from its own mistakes, it has little incentive to communicate outside on all potential mistakes even if it may gain in credibility in being quite open and transparent. This is why external evaluations are needed both to build institutional credibility and to form a judgment on the quality of any institution's operations. They should be commissioned and conducted in a fully independent way, outside institutions (or at least organized by them in a mutual, cooperative way so that peer pressure and peer review allow to counter the inevitable bias of having an institution judge its own actions). For example, the operations of the French Global Environmental Fund (FGEF), a Fund set up by the French government in parallel with the French participation in the Global Environment Facility (GEF) are thoroughly investigated before the decision to replenish the Fund, every three years. A team of independent auditors hired by the Board reviews the accounts, strategies and operations of FGEF.

There is a further dimension of accountability and judgment that could usefully be developed and that the current evaluation systems have not taken on so far, namely benchmarking of donors, multilateral as well as bilateral. Such benchmarking would be useful for two different sets of reasons. First, judgment of donor operations lack appropriate benchmarks. Quality of overseas development aid is better judged through comparison than in absolute terms. Benchmarking will better help inform taxpayers on whether their money was well used and whether it served useful purposes from their perspective. Second, benchmarking allows to compare the relative performance of donors and creates powerful incentives to improve efficiency in a world in which there is increasing competition among donors to collect development money, from a "market for aid" point of view, not only between public donors, but also between private foundations, NGOs, municipalities, etc.

May be even more than quality competition between donors, however, information on which donor does what best is also very valuable, as it may lead, within certain limits set by the global objectives of bilateral and multilateral assistance, to a possible natural division of labor between donors. There are already some interesting initiatives in that respect. The Consultative Group to Assist the Poor (CGAP), a consortium of 31 public and private development agencies that work toward expanding access to financial services for the poor in developing countries through micro-finance projects, took a very interesting aid effectiveness initiative in 2002 in organizing a peer-review of its member activities. Results were discussed in several meetings and identified donors that performed well and others that did not. Interestingly, at least one donor found to perform poorly decided to retire from microfinance operations as a result of this peer review. Such an approach obviously could be replicated in other areas.

2. Scientific impact evaluations

However well done and professional, current evaluations are not up to the task of measuring the actual impact of development projects and programs. Impact evaluation is a demanding task, because it requires both careful observation of direct and indirect results and careful assessment of attribution of these results to the operation that is under-evaluation. Control groups are needed, and the whole process of impact evaluation should be thought of very early on, as early as the operation to be evaluated is itself identified. Recent progress in scientific impact evaluation methods (be they random assignment methods or other rigorous ones) now make it possible to learn useful lessons about the actual development impact of some operations, and there is a welcome move toward developing this kind of approach. Impact evaluations are surely not a panacea, but they give a renewed dimension to evaluations, more akin to applied research than to the ex-post assessment of operations traditionally undertaken in evaluation units. It fulfills a fundamentally different role of building scientific knowledge, and it is worthwhile to encourage its development.

Decades of development assistance have brought home the fact that development is a complex and poorly understood process. This is a powerful reason for focusing on empirical approaches that will highlight the kind of actions and policies that achieve results and those who do not and why. In turn, such knowledge is necessary to allow for more effective selectivity within development institutions, allowing them to focus on what works and to avoid spending money on what does not. More than an evaluation of development institutions themselves, impact evaluation is a contribution to the provision of a global public good, namely knowledge on the development process.[7]

This public good character, together with the high cost involved in conducting scientific impact evaluations suggest that they will typically be under-supplied unless the coordination problem of who does what is solved. There is a further value added in coordination: better knowledge about what works in terms of development will have to be based not on empirical results from a single operation, but from comparing results from a number of operations in the same sector or with similar objectives. The way forward is setting up a system of cooperation between universities and development assistance donors toward joint impact evaluation, in which many donors take part, each of them contributing and all sharing the knowledge that is produced.

Available scientific methods, such as random evaluations, however, will work on some operations and much less on others. For cost as well as practicality reasons, not everything can undergo a scientific impact evaluation. Not everything is amenable to, say, random assignment like experimentation with drug use. For the very credibility of any exercise in scientific impact evaluation, therefore, it is crucial not to present it as a new religion, but rather as a contribution to better knowledge. For a start, what donors can usefully do is to initiate the process by selecting a few appropriate projects on which it is possible to build an operational cooperation between academic specialists and operational project officers, and by adopting a forthcoming, pragmatic approach. A number of initiatives deserve to be encouraged, notably the DIME project launched by the World Bank that proceeds along such lines.[8]

As argued above, however, when discussing the use of relevant knowledge in decision making, there will always be a need to keep a critical eye on the results from such scientific evaluations. It is unlikely that any scientific method of evaluation will allow to grasp all relevant factors in the interpretation of how a project or program fares in a given context, especially the institutional, human and societal dimension. What the method will help provide is a scientifically informed knowledge base on actions, not a book of recipes about development.

Moreover, it is useful to keep in mind that development is more about processes than results. An objective of "impact" evaluation should thus be to help measure incremental improvement rather than final impact. Even when positive impact is reached and documented, the question remains about sustainability. From this point of view, there is a continuum of concerns between process and impact evaluations.[9]

3. Concluding Remarks

Part of the difficulty in debating the evaluation function in donor institutions is that a number of different tasks are implicitly simultaneously assigned to evaluation: building knowledge on processes and situations in receiving countries, promoting and monitoring quality, informing judgment on performance, and, increasingly, measuring actual impacts. Agencies still need their own evaluation teams, as important knowledge providers from their own perspective and as contributors to quality management. But these teams provide little insight into our actual impacts, and, although crucial, their contribution to knowledge essentially focuses on a better understanding of operational constraints and local institutional and social contexts. All these dimensions of evaluations are complementary. For effectiveness and efficiency reasons, they should be carefully identified and organized separately: some need to be conducted in house, some outside in a cooperative, peer review or independent manner. In short, evaluation units are supposed to kill all these birds with one stone, while all of them deserve specific approaches and methods.

There is a need to substantially buttress scientific impact evaluations, because they clearly exhibit public goods characteristics in terms of providing empirical knowledge on development. They require increased cooperation among donors and joint action. A number of initiatives have been launched recently, notably under the aegis of the World Bank. The focus on developing impact evaluations, however, should not obfuscate the need to considerably improve the operational feedback from evaluation results and more broadly from all available, relevant knowledge to operations.

Knowledge is not a scientific good only. Careful impact evaluation is a complement, not a substitute, to the non scientific, empirical approach that is also part of knowledge building and quality control. As for judgment of performance, this is clearly not a mission for the donor agencies themselves: Their responsibility is to be accountable, namely to provide all available, accurate and unbiased information on their operations. Assessment of performance needs to be totally externalized and should not be even undertaken under a contract directly commissioned by the donors themselves, except through a carefully organized peer review system.

As a multilateral institution with a clear commitment toward improving aid effectiveness and researching on development processes, the World Bank should contribute placing the role and format of evaluations higher on donors' agendas. It has taken a leading role in developing impact evaluations and engaging other donors in co-organizing a publicly available knowledge base about the results from such evaluations. In a recent report presented to Paul Wolfowitz, President of the World Bank, in the spring of 2005, Birdsall and Kapur[10] notably recommend that the Bank should take the lead on independent evaluation of all aid spending. It should first, however, be also exemplary in taking part in existing peer reviews of donor operations in specific areas. Regretfully, the Bank did not participate in the CGAP peer review discussed above. Much is to be said in favor of a joint action by donors, alongside the CGAP example, to organize a rating of their operations in specific areas. As CGAP has demonstrated, it can provide very useful insights about what works and what does not and help donors become more selective in their operations.

Finally, development finance is not as much about picking out operations that work as about taking informed risks to discovering what works. Evaluations, along all the dimensions discussed above, are most useful to inform risk taking and decision making, rather than to act as substitutes to risk. The central, operational question is not whether operations similar to the one under consideration have been demonstrated to work in the past. In a dynamic, innovative, approach, it is rather whether all relevant knowledge has been called and taken into account so that the risk of development finance is carefully assessed.

Notes

1. I thank Pierre Forestier, Sebastian Linnemayr, Thomas Melonio, Jean-David Naudet and participants in the Center for Global Development symposium for useful comments, questions and suggestions. The usual caveat applies.

2. In particular, it is puzzling—and of questionable legitimacy—that we are seemingly putting more time and energy in trying to properly organize the evaluation of development projects than we seem to be in trying to assess the effectiveness of public policies in our own countries.

3. See www.worldbank.org/oed/.

4. For proposals along these lines, see William B. Savedoff, Ruth Levine and Nancy Birdsall, "When Will We Ever Learn? Recommendations to Improve Social Development through Enhanced Impact Evaluation," Consultation Draft, Center for Global Development, Washington D.C., September 15, 2005; and also Levine and Savedoff in this volume. Through its Development Impact Evaluation (DIME) project, the World Bank has also undertaken an exercise about encouraging scientific impact evaluations both in the Bank and in partner development institutions, with the aim of collecting and sharing results so as to improve knowledge on several aspects of development processes.

5. Eberhardt Reusse, *The Ills of Aid. An Analysis of Third-World Development Policies*, (Chicago: University of Chicago Press, 2002).

6. This is a problem akin to the one studied in the pioneering work by Richard Neustad and Ernest May, *Thinking in Time: The Uses of History for Decision Makers* (New York: The Free Press, 1986).

7. See for example Esther Duflo, "Evaluating the Impact of Development Aid Programmes: The Role of Randomised Evaluations," in *Development Aid: Why and How? Towards strategies for effectiveness*, Proceedings of the AFD-EUDN 2004 Conference, Notes and Documents No. 22 (Paris: French Development Agency, 2004).

8. The French Development Agency (AFD) has also decided to invest in scientific impact evaluation, starting with two projects, in microfinance and in health.

9. See the discussion in Smutylo, Terry (2001), "Crouching Impact, Hidden Attribution: Overcoming Threats to Learning in Development Programs", Draft Learning Methodology Paper, Block Island Workshop on Across Portfolio Learning, 22–24 May 2001, Ottawa: International development Research Centre.

10. Nancy Birdsall and Devesh Kapur, co-chairs, *The Hardest Job in the World. Five Crucial Tasks for the New President of the World Bank*, in this volume.

The Evaluation Agenda

by Ruth Levine and William D. Savedoff

The Bank's Success Depends on Knowledge

We will start with an obvious point: To succeed as an institution, the World Bank must succeed in its main business. Its main business is financing projects and programs that lead to better economic and social conditions than would have occurred without those projects or programs. A higher—and technically superior—definition would require that the returns for these projects and programs be at least a little better than their true economic costs. And a still more demanding standard might ask that the projects represent the *best* (most cost-effective) of all possible ways to achieve the same ends. But let's not be fussy here; let's just stick to the basic message that the Bank succeeds when poor people's lives improve because of the funding, technical expertise, accountability requirements or other dimensions of the Bank's lending and other instruments.

In contrast, the World Bank's success cannot be measured on the basis of whether the institution remains solvent, gets along well with NGOs, keeps employees happy, or fights corruption in-house and abroad. These are all probably necessary, but they're not sufficient. The Bank's success rests on whether it can make the lives of those who are sometimes referred to as the "ultimate beneficiaries" better off, in a meaningful way.

Ruth Levine, Center for Global Development
Ruth Levine is the director of programs and a senior fellow at the Center for Global Development. She is a health economist with 16 years of experience working on health and family planning financing issues in Latin America, Eastern Africa, the Middle East, and South Asia. At CGD, she manages the Global Health Policy Research Network. Before joining the Center, Ruth designed, supervised, and evaluated health sector loans at the World Bank and the Inter-American Development Bank.

William D. Savedoff, Social Insight
Bill Savedoff is a senior partner at Social Insight. In addition to preparing, coordinating, and advising development projects in Latin America, Africa and Asia, he has published books and articles on labor markets, health, education, water, and housing. He currently serves on the editorial board of *Health Policy & Planning* and as an editorial advisor to Transparency International.

Whether the Bank's projects and programs help borrowing governments to achieve good results for their citizenry depends in part on whether the programs are designed and implemented well. Take, for example, the case of a Bank-financed project aimed at improving enrollment, retention and learning outcomes of primary school students, which directs financing toward school construction, curriculum development, teacher training and new information systems in the Ministry of Education. Whether the project will achieve the desired results depends on whether the various project activities, from contracting for civil works to developing manuals for computer users, are conducted in a timely, cost-effective manner that takes into consideration local conditions. It also depends on whether the problem of low school attendance and performance can be solved with buildings, teacher skills, textbooks and computerized enrollment records. One would imagine that guidance on both of those questions, if not definitive answers, are within reach. Given the Bank's base of institutional experience—more than 50 years, across more than 100 countries and every sector, with billions of dollars of investments—a ready reserve of knowledge about what works should be available to inform critical design and implementation decisions. Indeed, it is just this type of asset that inspired the notion that the Bank could be a "knowledge bank."

The reality is quite distant from this idealized expectation, as any candid Bank employee will attest. The Bank appears to be structurally and perennially unable to learn.

The Bank Creates but Does Not Use Operational Knowledge

For operational questions, the Bank has shown itself to be reasonably good at generating "lessons"—but a mediocre student when it comes to applying them. The World Bank's Implementation Completion Reports (ICR) (prepared by staff or consultants at the conclusion of every project) and the broader sector studies generated by the Independent Evaluation Group (IEG), previously called the Operations Evaluation Department (OED), are replete with hard-won operational lessons, which are conveyed to the Bank's Board of Executive Directors in confidential documents. Classic and oft-repeated ICR conclusions include the inadvisability of establishing project management units that are isolated from line ministries; the importance of political commitment, managerial continuity, and timely follow-through when problems are detected; the need for operational research to inform mid-course corrections; the benefits of focused rather than multi-component "Christmas tree" investment programs; and the importance of developing a realistic financing strategy for the recurrent costs associated with the program. Though the same mistakes may be repeated from project to project, there's no doubt they are documented in detail each time.

The fact that these conclusions are oft-repeated is testimony to the limited impact that their documentation has on Bank practices and procedures, although they are ritualistically invoked at particular moments. It is striking, in fact, that one can often find essentially the same "lessons" in both the design document justifying the funding for a program and in the report after the funds have been spent. The design document may say that a "lesson learned" from similar operations is that project activities should be clustered so that the newly trained teachers are working in the rehabilitated schools that have the additional textbooks. Then, the ICR for the same project, seven years later, may say that results were disappointing because the project had to disperse investments widely, to maintain political support.

The reasons for this lack of learning about even the operational basics are many, and include everything from the extreme time pressure on staff, to the limited funding for disseminating the ICR results in a meaningful way, to the underlying incentives that result in oversized, unwieldy, unrealistically ambitious projects. Essentially no management attention is given to the sharing and application of this knowledge; and ICRs tend to be seen as bureaucratic by-products that yield no benefits to line managers or those who design and supervise the implementation of Bank projects.

The Bank Rarely Creates New Knowledge about What Works

While the Bank at least documents the operational lessons, it seldom generates the right kind of technical knowledge, or knowledge about what really works to achieve the desired impact. Technical lessons would come from analyses of how well similar projects achieved their aims in the past and would answer very basic questions that are at the core of project designs: What are the most effective (and cost-effective) ways to get girls to complete secondary school in rural Africa? What AIDS prevention strategies work to reduce the incidence of infection among mobile populations? Under what conditions do road-building projects reduce rural poverty?

On these sorts of questions, and the generation of knowledge about what works, the Bank's track record has been as wanting as virtually all other development institutions. It has systematically failed to even attempt to learn from one project or program how to get more and better results the next time around. Moreover, it has rarely undertaken and shared the type of data collection and analytic work that would contribute much needed light to the darkness of development assistance more generally.

The type of knowledge needed comes from impact evaluations, defined as evaluations that measure the results of an intervention in terms of changes in key variables (e.g., mortality, health status, school achievement and labor force status) that can be credited to the to the program itself, as distinguished from changes that are due to other factors. That is, they are evaluations that permit attribution of program-specific effects. At the Bank, as in the field of development more broadly, much emphasis has been placed on monitoring project performance and comparing before- and after-project conditions, while insufficient investments have been made in conducting rigorous impact evaluations that are necessary to tell us which interventions or approaches do and do not work.

This underinvestment in impact evaluation (and consequent undersupply of evidence about the relationship between specific types of investments and their effects) has a major, if painfully obvious, result: If we don't learn whether a program works in changing the well-being of beneficiaries, how do we know it's worth putting the money and effort into similar programs? If we don't bother to measure the results that are direct consequences of the specific program, how can we make a credible case for this, or any other type of expenditure of public funds?

This is the current scenario, lacking accumulated knowledge from impact evaluations. The typical World Bank social sector project is designed with a narrow range of inputs, sometimes generated by World Bank staff and consultants, and sometimes by the government receiving the loan or credit: a very detailed description and analysis of current (bad) conditions; guesses about the reasons for those bad conditions; a theory of change, or argument, that says "if you make these particular sorts of investments and institutional changes, the world will be a better place in these specific ways: fewer children will get sick and die, more children will go to primary school and learn something that will permit them to make a living in the future, and so forth. And not only will more of these good things happen because of the program's investments and institutional changes, but those good things would not have happened—or would not have happened so quickly—in the absence of this program."

Importantly, the dependence on this sort of argument is central to even broad "country-driven" programs that look much like budget support— for example, the Poverty Reduction Strategy Credits (PRSCs) are based on the notion that if you give the equivalent of block grants, or credits, to countries, they will allocate the resources in ways that reduce poverty. So while the Bank may not micromanage or "projectize" the spending, the successes of PRSCs or other forms of budget support is contingent, eventually, on the success of government decisions about how to spend those resources on public health, education and many other types of programs intended to reduce poverty and improve the life chances of the poor.

What is missing as an input into the design of most programs is a genuine evidence base to systematically support (or refute) that theory of change. Will those particular investments and institutional changes really make a positive difference, or do they just sound good? Have those investments resulted in the desired change before, in the same country or region, or elsewhere? We simply have no systematic information about this outside of a very narrow set of experiences that, primarily because of historical accident, have been well evaluated (e.g., conditional cash transfers in Mexico and Central America).

Why So Little Impact Evaluation?

Good impact evaluations are not a core part of the practice of international development. There are lots of very good reasons for this:

First, good impact evaluations require a degree of technical sophistication that is often lacking in the field of "applied development," where practitioners are accustomed to dealing with poor data and unfamiliar contexts. While many studies compare conditions before and after a project, such comparisons can be quite misleading without attention to other factors that might have also contributed to observed changes. For example, improvements in population health status might come from the introduction of new health care services, but they might also have been induced by rapid economic growth, migration, personal hygiene, climate change, or investments in infrastructure. Only by comparing observed changes among those who benefited from a project to some other control group is it possible to begin to disentangle how much of the effects can be attributed to the project or program itself.

Separating out the changes due to projects from changes due to other things is a complicated business, and to date the development community has been satisfied with weak alternatives, viewing more rigorous methods as inappropriate to the context of developing countries. Fortunately, advances in research methods and increasing capacity around the world to conduct such impact evaluations is beginning to surmount these technical difficulties.

Second, demand for the knowledge produced by impact evaluations tends to be spread out across many actors and across time. It is only at the moment of designing a new program that anything can be effectively done to start an impact evaluation. At that exact moment, program designers do want the benefit of prior research, yet have few incentives to invest in starting a new study. Paradoxically, if they do not invest in a new study, the same program designers will find themselves in the same position four or five years later because the opportunity to learn whether or not the intervention has an impact was missed.[1] Because information from impact evaluations is a public good, other institutions and governments that might have learned from the experience also lose when these investments in learning about impact are neglected.

Third, incentives exist at the institutional level to discourage conducting impact evaluations. Government agencies involved in social development programs or international assistance need to generate support from taxpayers and donors. Because impact evaluations can go both ways—demonstrating positive or negative impact—any government or organization that conducts such research runs the risk of findings that undercut its ability to raise funds.[2] Policymakers and managers also have more discretion to pick and choose strategic directions when less is known about what does or does not work. This can even lead organizations to pressure researchers to alter, soften or modify unfavorable studies, or to simply repress the results—despite the fact that knowledge of what doesn't work is as useful as learning what does. Similar disincentives to finding out "bad news" about program performance exist within institutions like the World Bank. For task managers, in fact, attempting to communicate negative results up the managerial "chain of command" can be one of the least career-savvy moves one can make.

Fourth, evaluation simply is not the central business of the Bank, and when material and human resources are stretched—as they typically are, even in the comparatively well-endowed environment of the Bank—short-term operational demands will override the longer-term, more strategic imperative of evaluation and learning. As one indication, resources spent to design and implement impact evaluations were not even recognized as a separate item in the World Bank's budgeting system until this year.

All of these reasons contribute to the situation observed today. For most types of programs, a body of scientific evidence about effectiveness is lacking. Bank task managers designing projects are left to their own devices. The general strategy is to observe that many other projects are based on the same theory of change, and on a plethora of anecdotes, "best practice"-style documentation to support a given program design, and reference to the writings of those who are regarded as particularly brilliant thinkers. This is "eminence-based decision making" rather than "evidence-based decision making."

A Smarter Future

Fortunately, many have recognized this problem, care about solving it, and are trying hard to find a way to do so.[3] Within the Bank, the IEG advocates for more resources for good evaluation, and makes heroic efforts to squeeze knowledge out of the experiences of projects that are conducted without baseline data, without comparison groups, sometimes without any impact indicators at all. In the past couple of years, the World Bank has created an initiative called the Development IMpact Evaluation (DIME) Initiative to: increase the number of Bank projects with impact evaluation components, particularly in strategic areas and themes; to increase the ability of staff to design and carry out such evaluations; and to build a process of systematic learning on effective development interventions based on lessons learned from those evaluations.[4]

The Bank identified five thematic areas to concentrate its current efforts at impact evaluation: school-based management and community participation in education; information for accountability in education; teacher contracting; conditional cash transfer programs to improve education outcomes; and slum upgrading programs. The Bank is also aiming to improve internal incentives to undertake more systematic development impact evaluations by explicitly recognizing these studies as a valued product in their own right.

This represents an important shift in the Bank's recognition of the value of impact evaluation—and particularly in the leadership of key individuals who have taken on this topic as a personal mission within the institution. The work of both IEG and the DIME deserve political and financial support.

But the chances are that this will not be enough. Even the best intentioned efforts, such as the DIME, will find it difficult over time to sustain their resources and maintain enthusiasm and rigor—particularly when some evaluations will inevitably show that many programs have been unsuccessful. In most institutions, internal offices that generate negative reports are subject to pressures to paint results in a positive light or, over time, find themselves increasingly isolated and with fewer resources.

A broader and bolder solution to the problem is required. Three central elements are required for a lasting and genuine solution to the problem of lack of knowledge about what works.

First, we need to use good evaluation methods to get answers to important questions. This means identifying the enduring questions, a process that would be done best if it were done in true partnership between developing countries and the range of institutions that provide development finance. The World Bank has made a start by identifying five thematic areas within its impact evaluation initiative. But the benefits of concentrating such studies around enduring questions across agencies and countries would be even greater. Surely there is an immense opportunity to learn by collaboration with different organizations that address similar health, education and other social problems in profoundly different ways.

Second, we need to use evaluation methods that yield answers. This means increasing the number of impact evaluations that use rigorous methods—such as random assignment and regression discontinuity—and applying them to a small number of programs from which the most can be learned. This does not obviate the need to continue process-oriented evaluation work, which can be tremendously informative to answer operational questions, but it does mean there is a new and large agenda for impact evaluation.

Third, while the overall set of important questions should be developed by the "interested parties" in development agencies and developing countries, the impact evaluations themselves need to be done independently of the major international agencies and borrowing country governments. Independent evaluations would be more credible in the public eye, and less subject to inappropriate pressures to modify results, interpretations or presentation. It is still important to work on changing the culture of the Bank in its entirety and all the myriad internal incentives to get projects done and implemented so that evaluation and learning become a regular part of all the Bank's activities. But the existence of an independent source of impact evaluation results—geared to a longer time frame and toward learning—will avoid many of the inevitable pressures to restrict the communication of bad news to higher levels of management.

A Proposed Solution

If leaders with vision in a few development agencies and a few developing country governments put their minds to it, a major improvement is within grasp. An international initiative could be established to promote more and better independent impact evaluations, undertaking, for example:

- Development of a shared agenda of "enduring questions" for selective evaluations around which multi-country/multi-agency evaluation could be done.
- Creation and dissemination of standards for methodological quality of impact evaluation.
- Provision of financial resources for design of impact evaluations.
- Provision of complementary resources for implementation of impact evaluations.
- Creation of a registry of impact evaluations.
- Dissemination of impact evaluation results.
- Development of a data clearinghouse to facilitate reanalysis.
- Support for the development of new and improved methods.

Appropriately, this would be a collective response to ensure supply of knowledge, a global public good in the truest sense. The ideal financing arrangements would be one based on sharing costs across those who benefit, or at least those agencies that choose to participate. Those resources should be additional to the current evaluation budgets, which have been pared down to subsistence level. Foundations and other private sector actors who see the long-term benefits and wish to facilitate generation of and access to knowledge might also be willing to provide start-up resources.

The question remains whether the Bank, which uses so little of its internally produced knowledge from ICRs and products of the IEG, would develop mechanisms to apply technical knowledge generated with the input of an independent facility. The answer to this may matter relatively little. If such knowledge were part of an international effort that disseminated findings broadly, those with whom the Bank works—counterparts who co-design projects with Bank staff—might find themselves well equipped with much more evidence about what works than they have today, and be able to shape the Bank's actions in a positive way.

The World Bank's participation in such an initiative would be truly win-win.The international community would benefit from the institution's expertise and access to knowledge from the Bank's tremendous portfolio of projects.The Bank would benefit from enhanced credibility and influence, as well as access to knowledge from other agencies' projects. Participating actively in the global process of learning what works is a natural role for the Bank to take on. Genuine success—making lives better—depends on it.

Notes

1. Ted O'Donoghue and Matthew Rabin "Doing It Now or Later," *The American Economic Review 89* (1999): 103–124.

2. Lant Pritchett, "It Pays to Be Ignorant: A Simple Political Economy of Rigorous Program Evaluation," *The Journal of Policy Reform 5* (2002): 251–269.

3. This section and those that follow are derived from discussions of the Evaluation Gap Working Group, and its final report, "When Will We Ever Learn? Improving Lives through Improved Impact Evaluation" (Center for Global Development, 2006). The ideas included here, however, are those of the essay authors, and not necessarily those of all working group members. For more information, see http://www.cgdev.org/section/initatives/_active/evalgap.

4. Information on DIME from personal communications with Francois Bourguinon, Paul Gertler and Ariel Fiszbein.

The World Bank: Buy, Sell, or Hold?

by Mark Stoleson

t seemed like a simple question, but the World Bank representative was visibly uncomfortable. Together with me was a delegation of investors visiting this small African country to see first-hand the micro-finance projects we had funded and to identify new development opportunities. We were visiting the World Bank's local offices to learn more about their activities and experience in the country. The Country Head was explaining how he planned to allocate his budget of over $100 million and highlighted one project to build cobble stone roads in the capital city. Knowing that the World Bank's mission is to reduce poverty, I assumed that building cobble stone roads would lead to a reduction in poverty. So, not being a development expert and almost thinking aloud, I asked our host: "How will these roads reduce the country's poverty?"

Surprisingly, he struggled to answer the question. After briefly discussing development theory, he finally stated that Bank staff on the ground do not have time to contemplate "ivory tower" notions such as the Bank's mission statement or overall goals but rather need to focus on the day to day business of managing their budgets and completing projects. But, I asked, if the projects do not reduce poverty, what is the point?

Only a few weeks before, World Bank President Paul Wolfowitz had emphasized the need to remedy the Bank's historically poor performance in Africa. He told Bank staff that "in the last 20 years, the number of people living in extreme poverty in Africa has doubled...in spite of roughly $200-300 billion in development assistance...[and] it's going to be hard to explain ourselves in 5 or 10 years if that picture remains the same. "In other words, results matter. Wolfowitz's comment seemed to imply the need for the Bank to focus not just on deploying capital and completing projects, but also on the overall "returns on

Mark Stoleson, Sovereign Global Development
Mark Stoleson is President of Sovereign Global Development. Please see
http://www.sov.com for more information about Sovereign Global.

investment," measured by the positive impact on the lives of people living in extreme poverty. In the office of the Country Head, however, concepts such as capital allocation and returns on investment seemed as far away as Washington DC.

An investor's view of the world bank

Following our meeting, I couldn't help but wonder how the World Bank might look, were it an investment opportunity. If this were a public company, I wondered, would I buy its shares? Would the World Bank meet the standards of performance to which investors such as Sovereign Global ("Sovereign") holds its investments?

Given the scale of resources entrusted to the World Bank, and the importance of its agenda, shouldn't someone enquire as to whether that institution is itself a wise investment? We came to this question with a perspective shaped both by experience in capital markets and emerging economies.

Sovereign has been investing in the international capital markets for over 20 years. During this time, the firm has provided capital to companies and governments from Asia and Africa to Latin America and Eastern Europe. Our investments have spanned many industries ranging from banking and energy to telecoms, power, and steel.

In every case, we have found that a good investment has certain characteristics: Firstly, it has a competitive advantage relative to its market, i.e., it is providing a product or service more effectively than any alternative organization. Secondly, it operates under the scrutiny of independent auditors or evaluators. Finally, it is accountable to its shareholders who ensure that it follows a set of coherent strategic goals. In simple terms we endeavor to measure the organization's competitiveness, transparency, and accountability.

Given these core conditions (though not guarantees) for success, how does the World Bank measure up? We ran the Bank through a basic set of questions we would ask when evaluating any investment opportunity.

Competitiveness: Is the Bank competitive at banking? The Bank's core customers—developing countries— increasingly are able to obtain financing from international debt capital markets. Still, the Bank persists in pursuing these customers: Over the past five years, 99 percent of its funds were loaned to countries that have investment grade or high-yield bond ratings.[2] Yet this core customer base turns to the Bank for only 1 percent of its total debt financing needs.[3] Any company that has a 1% market share amongst its target customer base has a dubious commercial rationale and future prospects.

You would think that given this loss of competitive standing, the Bank would shift more resources to an underserved marketplace, such as poor countries whose prospects for repayment are less certain. In fact, the share of such loans has gone from 40 percent of available funds in 1993 to 1 percent more recently.[4] What that suggests to us is that the Bank is chasing customers who do not want or need Bank funding, while increasingly ignoring the needs of countries that do.

In addition, the Bank's lending operations are unprofitable. Over the last 12 years the Bank has accumulated net losses of over $3 billion from its lending operations[5]—which could have supplemented the Bank's own borrowing and investment returns and provided the Bank with funds to make grants and concessional loans to the world's poorest countries. If the Bank were a better "bank" it would have more funds available for those who need it the most, but the opposite appears to be the case.

Is the Bank competitive at reducing poverty? The Bank's mission is "to fight poverty with passion and professionalism for lasting results." Presumably the mission is not only to fight, but also to win. After 50 years and $570 billion spent or lent, however, there is no conclusive data that demonstrates that the World Bank has made a meaningful impact on its primary mission. Poverty has declined in East and South Asia—but that is where World Bank development ideas and lending have been relatively small. Meanwhile, as highlighted by Adam Lerrick in recent testimony to the United States Senate, "The living standards of the poorest nations have stagnated and even declined as much as 25%."[6] The Bank has tremendous human and intellectual capital in the form of its experienced and committed staff. Why then has the Bank seemingly failed to deliver on its core mission of reducing poverty?

Transparency: Is the Bank a model of good governance? The Bank granted or lent $20 billion in 2005—not a huge amount by international banking standards, but certainly more than your average regional commercial bank. Yet it does not have a truly independent audit committee or employ outside auditors to objectively evaluate project performance. In the post-Enron, Sarbanes-Oxley world, it is incredible that a multi-billion dollar institution backed by taxpayer money is operating without independent oversight. If it were publicly traded on a U.S. stock exchange, the Bank's lack of an audit committee alone would cause it to be de-listed. Largely because of this blind spot, it is impossible for those either inside or outside the Bank to know whether it is effective or not, simply because it lacks any credible or objective metrics related to performance. Without measurable results there can be no accountability.

Accountability: Are the Bank's shareholders aligned in pursuing a sensible reform agenda? Shareholders with a common purpose can bring about governance reforms at under-performing companies. Reform will fail, however, if certain interests divide shareholders and conquer their common resolve. Or worse yet, if shareholders simply do not care about the returns on their investment, management will never improve performance. The World Bank does not lack its share of critics, both internal and external; many of those critics are the Bank's largest funders. Yet many of the Bank's financial backers either do not agree on a common agenda for reforming the Bank, or do not care to reform it in the first place. Either way, this flaw represents an abrogation of fiduciary responsibility by the Bank's shareholders to the Bank, to the taxpayers whose funds support the Bank's functions, and most of all, to the poor.

A solution from the private sector

These weaknesses would represent significant reasons not to invest in the World Bank. Its management and staff have an impressive and undeniable record of service and commitment to the cause of development, but the multiple and conflicting objectives of the Bank and its shareholders, combined with a total failure at self-governance and minimal involvement by shareholders, have made it impossible for positive "fundamentals" to emerge.

Any efforts to improve the Bank's competitive advantage must start with the creation of independent governance mechanisms and objective measures of success and failure. Without these measures, how would

Bank management and its shareholders discern what impact, if any, the Bank is really making?[7]

To make serious efforts toward upgrading its transparency and accountability, the World Bank, would benefit from adopting certain measures commonly used by public companies. Specifically, the World Bank could consider the merits of:

1. *Establishing an Independent Audit Committee.* Any effective audit committee is comprised of members that are truly independent. That means committee members could not accept any consulting, advisory, or other compensatory fee from the Bank, or be affiliated with the Bank or any of its entities other than as a member of the Board.

2. *Giving the Audit Committee Authority.* Independent audit committees generally report directly to the Board and have the authority and budget to hire their own counsel and consultants if necessary.

3. *Engaging Top Outside Auditors.* Audit committees are responsible for engaging and managing outside auditors. A World Bank audit committee could start by putting out for bid a multi-year, multi-million dollar auditing engagement that would draw in a qualified firm to audit the Bank's financial performance and projects while establishing proper internal controls so that the Bank's management team is equipped with the information they need to make sound decisions. The costs of a rigorous audit would be far outweighed by the benefits of transparency and accountability in addition to the valuable information the Bank would be able to provide to its management and the development industry as a whole about what works and what does not.

This proposal would offer many benefits. First, it would harness the inherent power of free market principles in fashioning new ways to evaluate development projects. Second, it would transform the World Bank from a laggard to a leader in accountability and transparency in the development community. And finally and most importantly, as the Bank responds to objective and accurate data about its performance, it will be able to make adjustments in its business model and operations so that it can more effectively deliver capital to the world's poorest communities.

For example, if the Bank were to recognize that larger and more focused grants have a greater likelihood of creating transformative change in a region, it would be able to restructure its grant-making to focus on such projects. If the Bank saw that its efforts must be combined within a larger coalition of NGO-led stakeholders on the ground, then that would be adopted as a preferred model. If the Bank saw that loans are still a credible instrument of development aid in certain cases, it could focus on that mechanism where appropriate and use grants elsewhere.

Moreover, by establishing credible accountability and governance measures, the Bank would finally address the weaknesses that have led to multi-billion dollar losses in loans. That would assure the Bank's shareholders—taxpayers from productive and wealthy nations—that the cause of development is "worth it" and would finally give the Bank the unified support and involvement of its shareholders. Performance, accountability and transparency are no longer optional in either the public or private spheres.

We know from experience that the most successful organizations constantly hold their performance up for analysis and criticism, and correct those problems as they emerge. Although there may be some resistance to an external audit of the World Bank, at the end of the day full transparency and accountability regarding its performance will free the Bank from its past, restore its credibility and relevance, and set it on a new course to more effectively change the lives of the world's poor. The Bank's mission is too important and its budget too large to accept anything less.

Notes

1. World Bank Town Hall Meeting Transcript, February 6, 2006.

2. See Adam Lerrick, "Has the World Bank Lost Control?" in this volume.

3. Id.

4. Id.

5. Id.

6. Adam Lerrick, "Is the World Bank's Word Good Enough?" Statement Presented to the Committee on Foreign Relations of the United States Senate, March 28, 2006.

7. See Ruth Levine and William D. Savedoff, "The Evaluation Agenda," in this volume.